God has promised to perseve~~~~~~~~~~~~~~~~~~~~~~~~~~~~~~~~~~~~ passive in the process. In fact, ~~~~~~~~~~~~~~~~~~~~~~~~~ is a real workout. It's a process that leads to what Aimee Byrd calls "theological fitness." With deep insight, biblical soundness, and practical illustrations, Aimee shows readers how to "hold fast . . . without wavering" (Heb. 10:23) all the way to the end.

—**Lydia Brownback**, Author, Speaker, and Blogger

The deeply informed Old Testament connections and the rich christological truth so famously given us in the book of Hebrews are intended to shape its very basic challenge to *hold fast* to Christ with a gospel-informed perseverance. This is just what Aimee does not miss, but drives the point home vividly in her distinctive, memorable, and popular style. A challenging yet enjoyable and valuable exhortation, and a pleasure to commend.

—**Fred G. Zaspel**, Pastor, Reformed Baptist Church, Franconia, Pennsylvania

If you think all exercise is drudgery, you're not doing it right. On the other hand, if building strength and stamina exhilarates you, you're more likely to persevere and achieve a greater measure of fitness. That's as true of our souls as it is of our bodies. If the pursuit of theological fitness sounds tedious to you, you're in danger of becoming a spiritual couch potato.

Aimee Byrd is here to help. She's the very best kind of theological sensei—an enthusiastic encourager, not a dour drill sergeant. She knows the joy of biblical and theological understanding, and it's an infectious delight. She shows how to gain and maintain theological fitness—and how to find great enjoyment in the exercise.

—**Phil Johnson**, Executive Director, *Grace to You* Radio Program

Like a good physical trainer pushes and encourages and equips and is clear about the rigors as well as the rewards of physical fitness, so Aimee Byrd, using the words of the writer of Hebrews, pushes and encourages and equips readers in *Theological Fitness*. In this Scripture-saturated book we are rightly warned of the rigors as well as promised the rewards of holding fast to Christ when we feel the burn and want to give up.

> **—Nancy Guthrie**, Bible Teacher; Author, Seeing Jesus in the Old Testament Bible Study Series

What a gem this book is—so full of encouragement and so honest and genuine. We see from Aimee what perseverance looks like on the ground, and at the same time her wonderfully practical and readable book is grounded in good theology.

> **—Thomas R. Schreiner**, Associate Dean, James Buchanan Harrison Professor of New Testament Interpretation, The Southern Baptist Theological Seminary, Louisville, Kentucky

# THEOLOGICAL
# FITNESS

# THEOLOGICAL FITNESS

## WHY WE NEED A FIGHTING FAITH

## AIMEE BYRD

P.O. BOX 817 • PHILLIPSBURG • NEW JERSEY 08865-0817

ISBN: 978-1-59638-995-3 (pbk)
ISBN: 978-1-59638-996-0 (ePub)
ISBN: 978-1-59638-997-7 (Mobi)

Portions of this book have been taken from the author's writings on her blog, www.housewifetheologian.com, and revised and adapted for this format.

Printed in the United States of America

**Library of Congress Cataloging-in-Publication Data**

Byrd, Aimee, 1975-
  Theological fitness : why we need a fighting faith / Aimee Byrd.
    pages cm
  Includes bibliographical references.
   ISBN 978-1-59638-995-3 (pbk.) -- ISBN 978-0-596-38996-0 (ePub) --
ISBN 978-1-59638-997-7 (Mobi)
  1. Christian women--Religious life. 2. Perseverance (Theology) I. Title.
  BV4527.B97 2015
  248.8'43--dc23
                           2015005417

To my mom and dad, Margie and Blaine,
who exemplify the life of fitness.

"I fear not the man who has practiced 10,000 kicks once, but I fear the man who has practiced one kick 10,000 times." —BRUCE LEE

# CONTENTS

# FOREWORD

It is a pleasure to commend the following book to you. Aimee Byrd is a friend, a cohost—with myself and Todd Pruitt—of the podcast *Mortification of Spin*, where she is the longsuffering target of the show's jokes (and indeed one who gives as good as she gets in that regard). She is also someone who feels passionately about theology and wants the church as a whole to love theology too.

But Aimee is not a theological brain on a stick. She is a wife and a mother. She is also a fitness fanatic, and in this book she uses the notion of fitness and physical training as a theme for exploring what it means to be a vibrant, theologically aware Christian. Indeed, the reader will find here not only great practical discussion of the everyday importance of theology but also lots of good advice on the benefits of physical fitness.

Of course, fitness was revolutionized for women in the '80s when Jane Fonda launched her workout videos and famously called on people everywhere to feel the burn. As I read this book, I could not avoid a mental image of Aimee barking out theological instructions to the beat of some ghastly '80s disco track. That may not be the most compelling image, but there is an analogy here: Fonda was a trailblazer who made it clear that being strong and fit was not a male preserve. Aimee is similar: one of a growing band of Reformed women who want to know theology and encourage others to do the same. She may not be demanding that we all feel the burn, but she is calling on us to understand what we believe in a thoughtful—indeed, a fit—way.

Carl R. Trueman
Paul Woolley Professor of Church History
Westminster Theological Seminary

# ACKNOWLEDGMENTS

An author labors away in front of a computer with an imaginary audience in mind, the readers. So I would like to extend my gratitude to every one of my readers taking the time to read my words. It is truly an honor.

The acknowledgments page gives me hope amongst all that is quickly changing in this world. Imagine if every product that you bought had an acknowledgments section. How many opportunities do we really have to thank the people who support our work? And authors can be a strange bunch, so we really do need to thank our loved ones for putting up with us as we try to work that manuscript out of our brain and present it to the public.

And so I thank my husband, Matt, for his ongoing encouragement in support, interview preps, editorial insights, and pretending that the house and I still look good on those busier writing days. Who knows the gratitude I owe him just for listening to all my ramblings? My kids, Solanna, Zaidee, and Haydn, just like to see their name in print, so I do thank them for being awesome. I am deeply grateful for the honor I had to teach the sermon-letter to the Hebrews to the women's Bible study in my last church, Pilgrim Presbyterian. Those women are a beautiful picture of theological fitness and perseverance. This book is a fruit that came from that study, along with the prayers of that amazing bunch. I am proud to run the race with you women. I should also mention that the concept of theological fitness first came to my mind when a Sunday school teacher and elder at

Pilgrim, Mike VanDerLinden, taught a lesson on Hebrews 12:1–2. Thank you to my previous pastor, Jerry Mead, for looking over chapter 10 for me. Many thanks go to Todd Pruitt for looking my manuscript over in detail and sharpening some of my ideas in responding to all my questions.

I grew up in a unique atmosphere when it comes to fitness. Our garage was converted into a dojo, where my dad taught martial arts and my mom taught aerobics to the neighbors. Mom eventually opened a gym, and dad was also in the Secret Service for a while. This experience has led to a mind-set and discipline that crosses over well to the field of theological fitness. It has also given me great stories and analogies to use in discussing our conditioning in the Word of God. My parents are an exceptional gift from the Lord. I also need to thank my dad, as well as my brother, Luke, for passing along their awesome nunchuck skills for the book trailer. Luke is to be thanked for producing the video as well.

My experience with P&R has been a true delight. Special thanks go to Ian Thompson, Bryce Craig, and Amanda Martin for meeting with me to determine what shape this book would take. It's like a family over there, and I enjoy working with everyone. I very much appreciate all the labor—from the editorial work, the art department (who has to put up with my crazy suggestions), my project manager to the marketing team, and my sensei–project manager, Aaron Gottier. And after having the pleasure of visiting the P&R warehouse, I am grateful to the men who box up the books and ship them out. And payroll, can't forget payroll.

Also important to the formation of this book are the readers of my blog.[1] I've tested some of the content of this book on Housewife Theologian and have so benefited from the encouragement and sharpening I continually receive from my readers.

1. Aimee Byrd, *Housewife Theologian* (blog), Alliance of Confessing Evangelicals, http://www.housewifetheologian.com.

# INTRODUCTION

What is perseverance? We Christians like to use this word, but do we really know what it means? If we are talking about the Christian life (and we are), then we undergo a transformation in persevering to our goal. We begin the faith as babes in Christ, and we are steadfastly pressing forward to that great day when we will see his face and reign with him in the new heavens and the new earth. And when that day comes, we will not be as we are now. We will be holy. We will be changed. And so, as we persevere, we are being prepared for holiness. We are being made like Christ.

When we say, "I am a Christian," what do we mean by this profession? This is a very important question. In fact, I would like to propose that our answer to this question, and our ability to proactively cling to a proper confession of what we believe, is directly connected to our perseverance in the Christian life. All Christians need to know what they are persevering for, whether it is through a fiery trial or the mundanity of everyday living. This entails a tenacity to grasp what is true about the person and work of Jesus Christ. I call it *theological fitness*.

I realized this as I was teaching a women's Bible study on Hebrews. This sermon-letter[1] was written to exhort the intended first audience of Jewish believers to persevere in the Christian faith and not to turn back to their old covenant

1. For a good explanation of the genre of Hebrews as a sermon-letter, see Dennis E. Johnson, "The Epistle to the Hebrews as an Apostolic Preaching Paradigm," chap. 6 in *Him We Proclaim* (Phillipsburg, NJ: P&R, 2007), 167–97.

sacrificial system and ceremonies. Of course, in his providence, it is also God's Word to us. Indeed, Hebrews gives us all a better understanding of the true Prophet, Priest, and King to which all others were only a type and shadow. It is a very theological sermon. Theology is merely the study of God, knowing God. After studying all the indicatives of who God is and what he has done in Christ, I was captivated with a particular imperative that the preacher to the Hebrews lays out in order to press the reader to perseverance: "Let us hold fast the confession of our hope without wavering, for he who promised is faithful" (Heb. 10:23).

That's it. That's how you persevere. This exhortation is the center of three "let us" statements that the author is applying to the Hebrews after teaching how the person and work of Christ gives us direct access to God through a new and better covenant. And it really sums up the message of perseverance that is the theme of the whole sermon-letter.[2] Before this, the writer carefully gives us a detailed theology, thoroughly explaining the Christian confession of hope. And what imperative follows to encourage us in faithful perseverance throughout the sermon-letter? Hold on to it—not just cavalierly, but hold fast! Our exhortation is to hold fast to our confession. For the rest of the sermon, this exhortation is expounded. Are you tempted to backslide? Hold fast! Are you being persecuted? Hold fast! Through suffering, fear, and chastisement, and in the ordinary, everyday life of faith and obedience, we are encouraged to hold fast. It may sound like an easy adage, but my goal in this book is to show you that it is a workout. And this kind of workout, this exhortation, in fact, promotes a theological fitness.

Think about it. The author to the Hebrews is telling us to hold fast to a theological statement. What does that even mean? And what does it take? How does this help us to persevere?

2. "The author's plea is summed up in Hebrews 10:23" (Richard D. Phillips, *Hebrews* [Phillipsburg, NJ: P&R, 2006], 9).

## WHAT DOES THAT EVEN MEAN?

It means that we need to intimately "know what we believe and why we believe it."[3] In other words, it means that you need to be a good theologian. Unfortunately, many evangelicals today seem to have an aversion to theology. Studying God's Word and learning about our Creator and Redeemer require exertion. After all, we aren't striving just to learn *about* God, but to *know* him intimately. All relationships require effort. But how can we compare knowing the one and only God to any other relationship? It's overwhelming. How are we even worthy to learn?

And yet our great God has spoken. He has condescended to communicate to us, revealing his character in a covenant treaty. The words that God has carefully preserved about his plan of redemption, his sovereign holiness, goodness, love, justice, amazing mercy, and grace, are taken for granted. The average American owns more than three copies of the Bible,[4] many of which are collecting enough dust to write the word *damnation* across the cover, as Charles Spurgeon so eloquently put it.[5] Think about it: the authoritative Word of God, collecting dust. To persevere, we need to know the confession of our hope, and we can't do that with a dusty Bible.

## WHAT DOES IT TAKE TO KNOW GOD?

It takes holding fast to the truth he reveals about himself in his Word. And that takes fitness. When we hear the word *fitness*, we most likely apply it to someone who is in good physical health. To be fit is to be competent, to have the skill needed for

---

3. This is the motto of White Horse Inn. See "About Us," White Horse Inn, accessed March 6, 2015, http://www.whitehorseinn.org.

4. Stoyan Zaimov, "Poll: Americans Own Many Bibles, But Rarely Read Them," *The Christian Post*, March 21, 2012, http://www.christianpost.com /news/poll-americans-own-many-bibles-but-rarely-read-them-71823/.

5. Charles H. Spurgeon, "The Bible," in *Spurgeon's Sermons*, vol. 1–2 (repr., Grand Rapids: Baker, 1996), 33.

the task at hand. A lifestyle of fitness and good health is highly promoted in our culture for both the quality and length of life. But we know that, as hard as we work to be physically healthy, it is a fading reality. So if physical fitness is valuable even though our bodies are aging and wasting away, how much more valuable is a spiritual, theological fitness? "So we do not lose heart. Though our outer self is wasting away, our inner self is being renewed day by day" (2 Cor. 4:16).

And yet many people have an aversion to fitness. We all want to have good health, right? So what's the problem? The problem is that there is something always working against us in our fight to be healthy, whether it is in a physical pursuit of fitness or in a vigorous effort to know God. John Owen explains that this command in Hebrews to hold fast insinuates an opposing force, a "great danger" even. "To 'hold fast' implies the putting forth our utmost strength and endeavors in the defense of our profession, and a constant perseverance in so doing."[6] Holding fast to our confession of hope requires fight. One thing is for sure, we cannot hold fast to a confession of hope that we know little about. Faith is a gift of God, but faith is a fighting grace. *Theological fitness, then, refers to that persistent fight to exercise our faith by actively engaging in the gospel truth revealed in God's Word.* It isn't just a remembering of some Bible verses about God, but a trust in his promises that motivates us in holy living.

God's Word cannot be ignored. We must wrestle with it. This takes a level of theological fitness and stamina. There are some great illustrations of physical fitness given in Scripture to explain this theological fitness, as I have named it. In Hebrews alone, the Christian is compared to a marathon racer and a combatant in the Grecian Olympics (Heb. 12:1–2, 12). We see in Philippians 1:27–29 an image of military combat training that the Grecian Olympics borrows from for competitive pur-

6. John Owen, *Epistle to the Hebrews* (Grand Rapids: Kregel, 1968), 200.

poses. Paul also talks about running a race to win the prize in 1 Cor. 9:24–27. These are all exhortations to a theological fitness in perseverance.

Neither Paul nor the writer to the Hebrews was writing to an audience full of athletes, and neither am I. But the illustrations are used anyway because they help us to understand that the Christian life also takes training, exercise, and fight to persevere. I don't care if you are physically fit as much as I care about your theological fitness. So I am writing to every Christian who would like to have a better understanding of perseverance by having a better understanding of who God is and what he has done.

## HOW DOES THIS HELP US TO PERSEVERE?

I am suggesting that our perseverance in the Christian faith is connected to our theological health. And yet our Hebrews 10:23 verse gives us great news. We persevere not because of our own faithfulness, but because he who promised is faithful. Indeed, we see that Christ has already gone before us in the race and secured our victory. Only Jesus had the fitness for the work of our salvation. But he has now qualified us for the race of the Christian life. This is encouraging! How could we not want to learn all there is to know about our great Savior and Victor? And the more we learn about our God, the more our theological fitness level is strengthened.

Our theology shapes the way we live. What we believe about who God is, who we are, and what he has done will affect our everyday thinking and behavior. As we learn about our Creator and Redeemer, our desire is to be like Christ. And this is God's promise to his people. But do we really believe this as we are hitting our alarm clocks, wondering if there is any way we can afford just seven more minutes of sleep? Do we really believe that we are going to be like Christ when all is said and done? And how do we get to that point?

## WHAT CAN YOU EXPECT?

What I hope to do in this book is to further explain theological fitness and to encourage you in perseverance by unpacking all the rich elements in this great verse, Hebrews 10:23. I've broken down the verse into five parts, each with two chapters expanding upon the idea of that segment. There are questions at the end of each chapter that make this book easy to use for a small-group study. And yet I don't want to just rip Hebrews 10:23 out of its context to do a study on perseverance and theological fitness. I want to raise this verse up while recognizing all the rich strands of context that surround it in the sermon-letter to the Hebrews. So you will notice that while I certainly am going to be using other Scriptures for this workout—I mean study—I will also be borrowing much from this sermon-letter on perseverance.

We may be well aware of our physical fitness levels. Whether they are good, fair, or terrible, we certainly understand the need for health. But our fitness levels reveal our readiness in other areas as well. Are you aware of your mental fitness or emotional fitness levels? These are analogies that I will use as well to compare with my teaching on theological fitness.

How do we hold on to a confession? And what is our hope? Is this something that we do alone? What happens if we falter? These are questions that this book will answer. Our hope is real because our God is faithful. And yet every Christian struggles with this simple truth. I know how hard it is to begin a workout. Sometimes we just don't feel like doing what it takes for fitness. But like I said, faith is a fighting grace. I'm afraid that we tend to associate it with suffering and trial, or maybe even just getting by. And who wants to talk about that? Do you wake up each morning psyched to persevere through your day? Or do you wake up hoping to survive through it? I think we often think of perseverance as passive endurance.

I hope to change that.

I propose that perseverance is an exciting exhortation for every Christian. My goal is for this book to serve you like your favorite song that gets you pumped up for your next event. Every Christian will persevere in the Christian life. But perseverance takes fight, and fighting is not passive.

You may be going through a hard time in your life right now. Maybe you are struggling in a difficult relationship, dealing with the death of a loved one, or trying not to let an illness get the best of you. Many of us are just trying to continue on in our ordinary lives. A better understanding of the doctrine of perseverance will motivate us to face it all with a sense of purpose and joy. I invite you to take up some theological fitness training with me as I unpack this one amazing verse along with the great metaphor that physical fitness lends to theology.

# PART 1

# "LET US"

# | 1 |

# TOUGHEST EVENT
# ON THE PLANET[1]

Our key verse on theological fitness, Hebrews 10:23, opens with "*Let us* hold fast the confession of *our* hope without wavering, for he who promised is faithful." Right away we see that this exhortation is to the covenant community of believers, not something that we do in isolation.

Have you heard of the Tough Mudder? It is a hardcore, ten- to twelve- mile challenge. British Special Forces designed the twenty-five military-style obstacles that make up the course. The task seems insurmountable, as the website boasts that it will "test your all around strength, stamina, mental grit, and camaraderie."[2] Indeed it will. Seriously, watch the video footage on their website. Those are the images I had in my head while teaching a Bible study lesson on Hebrews 11:13–16:

> These all died in faith, not having received the things promised, but having seen them and greeted them from afar, and having acknowledged that they were strangers and exiles on the earth. For people who speak thus make it clear that they are seeking

1. The slogan for Tough Mudder. "Press Room," Tough Mudder, accessed November 1, 2013, http://www.toughmudder.com/press-room.
2. Tough Mudder Perth (Team SXF), Facebook post, October 27, 2013, https://www.facebook.com/events/245926515552094/.

a homeland. If they had been thinking of that land from which they had gone out, they would have had opportunity to return. But as it is, they desire a better country, that is, a heavenly one. Therefore God is not ashamed to be called their God, for he has prepared for them a city.

My brother, Luke, assembled a team from his Mixed Martial Arts academy to compete when the Tough Mudder rolled into Frederick, Maryland. The first obstacle was called the *Arctic Enema*—pretty much a pool of ice water that you have to swim through. The *Boa Constrictor* course consists of cold, muddy pipes that you crawl up and downhill through, only to then progress to a sloppy, muddy barbwire course on the other end. Many of these obstacles are impossible without help. The *Everest* is a quarter-pipe wall coated in mud and grease. I don't even think the American Ninja Warriors can make it over this wall alone. And if I had to pass through the *Electroshock Therapy* (yes, you get shocked!) alone I would be rocking back and forth in the corner crying.

You might be thinking, "This is totally what those Mixed Martial Arts kind of people would feel they have to do to prove their toughness." Maybe, but there is much more to it than that. Here is a part of their philosophy on the website: "But Tough Mudder is more than an event, it's a way of thinking. By running a Tough Mudder challenge, you'll unlock a true sense of accomplishment, have a great time, and discover a camaraderie with your fellow participants that's experienced all too rarely these days."[3] This is exactly what I heard from all the participants. There's something about focusing on a goal together, overcoming every obstacle on the way.

Tough Mudder isn't about finishing first, either. The team stays with their weakest link, helping one another to finish all together. The event has raised over six million dollars for the

3. Ibid.

Wounded Warrior Project. You see wounded warriors competing alongside, prosthetic legs and all. Pretty cool.

The above Scripture from Hebrews highlights the fact that God's people are also focusing on a common goal that changes our perspective. Particularly when discussing what it means to be a pilgrim with my Bible study group, I thought of this obstacle course. Pilgrims have a destination, and they must lay aside any distraction that hinders them from reaching their goal. There are many obstructions on our heavenward journey. If our focus is on the barriers, we may want to turn back. But believers don't even have that option. Like the Tough Mudders, we have a completely different way of thinking. Our minds must be focused on the eternal promises in Christ. First we see them, then we are assured of them, and so we embrace them, confessing our identity in Christ.[4]

## UNITY IN STRIVING FOR THE PROMISE

Paul gives a similar analogy to my Tough Mudder illustration in his letter to the Philippians. Appealing to the status of Roman citizenship that is valuable to the Philippians, as well as to the high population of soldiers inhabiting Philippi as a military town, Paul uses language that will invoke a passionate response.

> Only let your manner of life be worthy of the gospel of Christ, so that whether I come and see you or am absent, I may hear of you that you are standing firm in one spirit, with one mind striving side by side for the faith of the gospel, and not frightened in anything by your opponents. This is a clear sign to them of their destruction, but of your salvation, and that from God. For it has been granted to you that for the sake of Christ

4. See Arthur W. Pink, *An Exposition of Hebrews* (Grand Rapids: Baker, 2004), 719.

you should not only believe in him but also suffer for his sake. (Phil. 1:27–29)

Dennis Johnson shone some light on this passage in his commentary on Philippians. "Behind our English version's 'let your manner of life be' (ESV) is a single Greek verb that has *citizen* at its core. The Greek word for *city* is *polis*, from which we get the word *politics*."[5] He explains how Paul normally refers to the Christian walk in an exhortation such as this, but we see him use a word here that appeals to behaving worthily of the citizenship to which you have been granted. Philippians esteemed their status as a colony of Rome because it came with great privileges. Those with Roman citizenship were guaranteed due process in a Roman court trial and considerable exclusion from certain taxes.[6] Johnson also points out that in an area full of retired soldiers and active-duty troops, the language Paul uses such as "*standing firm* in one spirit, with one mind *striving side by side* . . . and not frightened in anything by your opponents" would stir up "vivid combat memories," the readers knowing that "steadfast courage and unity were crucial to victory."[7]

As Paul is drawing on the Philippian pride of citizenship and the connection that has to service as a soldier, he is invoking an image of what it is like to be a citizen of Christ's heavenly kingdom. First, he emphasizes the necessity of God's Spirit as the "divine Guardian of our unity of soul and mind."[8] With this in mind, Paul then gives a great illustration of theological fitness in the phrase "strive side by side." Johnson provides the background of the derivation of this phrase.

> "Striv[e] side by side" is derived from a root that sometimes refers to athletic competition. (The birthplace of the original

5. Dennis E. Johnson, *Philippians* (Phillipsburg, NJ: P&R, 2013), 88–89.
6. Ibid., 89–90.
7. Ibid., 89.
8. Ibid., 92.

Olympics lay some distance south of Philippi in Achaia.) Yet ancient Greek athletics developed out of military training for combat, as we still see today in sports such as the javelin, the hammer, the discus, and wrestling. Here, Paul is thinking in terms of mortal combat. He paints the picture of an advancing line of Roman legionnaires, their long shields forming both a seamless wall before them and a "roof" over their heads against the enemy's arrows and spears.[9]

What an amazing picture of Christ's church! There is no looking out for oneself. There is no running ahead or leaving anyone behind. It is active recognition of interdependence upon one another in perseverance. This kind of unity requires humility and confidence in the Lord. Paul is admonishing a church that has been wrapped up in selfish bickering in reaction to persecution and false teaching. He is reminding them of their status in a much more marvelous citizenship. This is a call to behave according to who they are. There is an enemy, and Jesus Christ is exactly whom both the Philippians and we can draw upon for soldiering ahead. As we recognize our status as Christ's church, there is no room for independent perseverance.

> But citizen-soldiers who serve heaven's King, Jesus, will not compete as rivals or withdraw in introspective self-pity, each licking his or her own wounds and ignoring others' pain. Rather, their costly compassion for others, their humble honoring of others, will reflect the humility and compassion of the Lord and Savior who reigns in their true city. *Selfless solidarity!*[10]

Christian perseverance isn't a self-seeking fight. We strive together and honor one another, even when it is uncomfortable and difficult—especially when it is uncomfortable and difficult. We invest in one another because of the one who invested in

9. Ibid.
10. Ibid., 92–93.

us. And we hold fast to our hope in the covenant community of the church. Part of knowing God (theology) is knowing his bride, the church.

It's funny. People dress up for these Tough Mudder events. The teams who enter to compete together usually pick a theme to identify themselves and promote unity. My brother's crew decided to all dress like superheroes. I'm sure this is much different from the Philippian soldiers' uniforms. As ordinary, modern-day Christians, we may not be in funny costumes, but there should still be a sense in which we seem like strangers to the watching world. Our royal status in Christ's kingdom may not be worn ostensibly, but as we progress in our journey we are being transformed and prepared for eternal glory. How amazing is that?

## ORDINARY (MEANS) VS. EXTRAORDINARY (GRACE)

God didn't send us out alone as strangers and pilgrims on this earth. He has the entire church as the body of Christ, sisters and brothers in the Lord, who accompany us. He even set aside the first day of every week for worship together, a glimpse of what is to come. And so the preacher to the Hebrews labors to explain why they can now draw near to God in worship. His first "let us" imperative is "let us draw near with a true heart in full assurance of faith, with our hearts sprinkled clean from an evil conscience and our bodies washed with pure water" (Heb. 10:22). Immediately following our exhortation to hold fast the confession of our hope, the writer of Hebrews sandwiches it with another imperative for the church:

> And let us consider how to stir up one another to love and good works, not neglecting to meet together, as is the habit of some, but encouraging one another, and all the more as you see the Day drawing near. (10:24–25)

As we wait for the approaching day of our Lord's return, believers are given something quite extraordinary. On the first day of every week, we are called to gather together for corporate worship. This worship service seems pretty ordinary. We live in an entertainment-driven culture that is saturated in the latest technology. With the many vying messages fireworking on our phones, computer screens, televisions, and other devices, our attention spans have actually shrunk. We expect crisp, visual interfaces and easily scanned information. As Nicholas Carr so aptly put it, "Once I was a scuba diver in the sea of words. Now I zip along the surface like a guy on a Jet Ski."[11] The thought of singing along with a mediocre ensemble of instruments and voices, and then listening to a twenty-minute or longer sermon, may sound unappealing to a culture accustomed to such extraordinary means of communication. And with the five-star-restaurant–worthy recipes that I can pull up on Pinterest, broken bread and a sip of wine may not seem worth my time.

God has ordained very ordinary means to communicate extraordinary grace while the world uses extraordinary means to communicate ordinary, humdrum data. A study done by Retrevo interviewing one thousand people indicates that 48 percent of us check Facebook before getting out of bed.[12] So eager to get the latest update, many don't seem to mind being interrupted during a meal, in the bathroom, or even during an intimate moment. Facebook and Twitter seem to be a preferred means to take in the daily news, according to this study. And what is the worthy information that we are running to our gadgets for? One quick glance of my Facebook newsfeed is showing me a picture of a friend's coffee drink, some people complaining about the weather, a handful of worthy articles to share (and

11. Nicholas Carr, *The Shallows: What the Internet Is Doing to Our Brains* (New York: W. W. Norton & Company, 2010), 7.
12. See Sharon Gaudin, "Social Networking Addicts Updating from Bed, Bathroom," Computerworld, March 7, 2010, http://www.computerworld.com/s/article/9172378/Social_networking_addicts_updating_from_bed_bathroom.

funny ones too), an announcement that a friend's son received his driving license, as well as numerous selfies and advertisements. Pretty ordinary.

And yet the actual percentage of people who will get out of bed for a worship service as regular attendees may be less than 20 percent.[13] Do the means of grace that God has instituted seem too ordinary to get out of bed for? Are we welcoming interruptions by our social networks while turning a blind eye to the weekly interruption of the age to come into this age—an age that is wasting away? That is in a sense what is happening when we gather for corporate worship—the future is interrupting the present.

While our spectacular, shiny devices mediate our friends' latest status updates to us, Jesus Christ and all his benefits are conferred to us through the preached Word and the sacraments. Hebrews tells us that Jesus is the Mediator of a better covenant that is established by better promises (8:6). We have direct access to God through Christ's priestly service. Not only that, but in him we make up the living temple of God, "mediating God's presence to the world."[14] The church is a living picture of extraordinary grace. We are a body full of helpless sinners, who have been rescued and redeemed and now embody the Spirit of our Savior himself! Yes, we are individually given the Holy Spirit as a sign and a seal of our new creation in Christ, but together as his church we are his beloved bride that he will come for on that approaching day.

As our weeks bombard us with updates through the means of our extraordinary devices, we may begin to think that we are receiving extraordinary information. But when we are

13. See Kelly Shattuck, "7 Startling Facts: An Up Close Look at Church Attendance in America," CHURCHLEADERS, accessed March 6, 2015, http://www.churchleaders.com/pastors/pastor-articles/139575-7-startling-facts-an-up-close-look-at-church-attendance-in-america.html/5.

14. G. K. Beale, "The Temple and the Church's Mission" (lecture, Christ Reformed Church, Anaheim, CA, March 30, 2007), available online at http://links.christreformed.org/realaudio/20070330a.mp3.

called together as a people to a set-apart space, we hear truly amazing news. We need to hear the gospel preached because this good news is completely outside of ourselves. And not only is the message powerful, but the Word itself is living and active, revealing our hearts (see Heb. 4:12). I may be able to present my best to you on all my social profiles, but before God I am completely exposed. The law of his Word undresses my faux self-importance and self-righteousness, and then the gospel graciously clothes me in the righteousness of Christ. I find that all the little stories I think are significant throughout the week are put in perspective as I'm recast into the divine drama revealed in Scripture.[15] Michael Horton articulates it so well: "Created by speech, upheld by speech, and one day glorified by speech, we are, like the rest of creation, summoned beings, not autonomous. We exist because we have been spoken into existence, and we persist in time because the Spirit ensures that the Father's speaking, in the Son, will not return void."[16]

## HELP TO HOLD ON

Our verse could have just begun with "Hold fast the confession of your hope," but it doesn't. It begins, "Let *us* hold fast the confession of *our* hope." When you think of holding fast to something, it doesn't really sound like a group activity, does it? But there is something about Christ's body, the church, that makes all the difference. Jesus gave us the church as a gift that glorifies him and produces Christlikeness in us. We can be confident that theological fitness, that persistent fight to exercise our faith by actively engaging in the gospel truth revealed in God's Word, is not something we participate in alone. The church

15. "Holy time (Sabbath) and holy space (temple) provide the coordinates for the covenant people" (Michael S. Horton, *People and Place: A Covenant Ecclesiology* [Louisville: Westminster John Knox Press, 2008], 262).
16. Ibid., 61.

helps us to hold on through encouragement and exhortation. In that way, we hold on together.

We see in our verses above that encouragement is a major role as our calling in the body of Christ. I thought about that verse when I picked my eldest daughter up from volleyball conditioning last year. Solanna had just begun conditioning for her second season as a high school volleyball player. But at almost fourteen years old, she was barely five feet tall. It can be challenging when she is playing sports up against her full-grown friends. Solee did make the high school volleyball team as an eighth grader and had a great season. During the off-season, I tried to encourage her to work out with me to keep her fitness level up. And with a little prodding she would fit in a workout here and there.

Once conditioning started up again for her as a freshman, I wasn't sure how she was going to do with the hour and a half of fitness. Being smaller, Solee had to work a bit harder to do some of these workouts. When I picked her up from her first day back to conditioning, Solanna said she had held her own pretty well with the upperclassmen. They were surprised that she could do the box jumps that many of them could not. "How does that little girl get up there?" But the second evening when I picked her up, Solee was smiling from ear to ear with some news. "Mom, we had to do the six inches today [this is where you lay on your back and raise your feet six inches for as long as you can—a killer on the abs!], and I lasted the longest, even beating the varsity girls!" It turns out that my girl held on for five minutes with her feet raised. Five minutes! I challenge you to try it for thirty seconds.

I was super impressed at Solanna's drive to hang in there. It was so rewarding to see her proud, accomplished smile as I shouted, "Perseverance!" with my victory arm raised in the air. I keep telling the kids that perseverance takes fight, and fighters need to train. This small victory was affirming of this very truth.

But it wasn't just training during the off-season that helped Solanna to persevere. Solee said her legs were shaking like crazy and she really wanted to give up. However, she had a friend there who had already gone down, and she was encouraging Solanna to hold on. When it was down to three girls, Solee's friend was telling her whose legs were shaking and was cheering, "You've got this!" She kept encouraging her not to quit.

Solanna had something that helped her to hold on, similar to what Christ gives us. She had an encourager. This is just what the writer to the Hebrews was emphasizing in our verses above. Following our call to hold fast, we are told to encourage and exhort the body of believers. Solee's friend did both in a mere fitness challenge, and it made all the difference. She encouraged her with "You got this," and she exhorted her, "Don't give up!"

Christ gives us a whole body of encouragers with whom we run the race of the Christian life together. What a blessing! But we have much more to equip us in perseverance than my daughter did in her fitness challenge. Christians are exhorted to hold fast the confession of our hope without wavering because he who promised is faithful. Solee didn't have a confession of hope; she had to depend on her own abilities while she was going through the pain. But Christians can hold on through adversity because we have the fitness of Jesus Christ who went before us. And not only do we get his Holy Spirit as a helper, but we are part of a body of worshipers. Why would we neglect this wonderful gift?

Solee's small triumph was a reminder to me to be an encourager in the Lord. All of us need encouragement. A girl on her team last year said to me, "Solee may be the smallest girl on the team, but I think she's the strongest." Sometimes we forget to encourage those who we know to be strong because, well, they are strong. We don't think they need it. That couldn't be further from the truth! The strong often need all the more encouragement because they usually carry a heavier load. My little girl has big strength, but it was her encouraging friend who helped her to persevere to the end.

## AND AGAIN

Do you ever get a bit turned off when authors begin repeating themselves in a book? Perhaps you have felt this way in reading this book. If that is the case, I thank you for persevering this far. The thing is, we need things repeated to really learn. We actually have to *overlearn*, so that we can remember and then possibly teach others. This exhortation to the church is so important that the preacher to the Hebrews finds it worth repeating several times in this one sermon. In the midst of a warning against falling away from God, we see this accompanying call again:

> But exhort one another every day, as long as it is called "today," that none of you may be hardened by the deceitfulness of sin. For we have come to share in Christ, if indeed we hold our original confidence firm to the end. (3:13–14)

Again, we see this connection between theological fitness—that is, holding firm to our confession—and the love and unity for each other in the church. Notice that this isn't merely a Sunday-morning duty. We are called to exhort one another every day! I am feeling convicted right now as I'm writing these words. That is a lot! It sets off a list in my head of people I should call, send cards to, or invite over for a visit. Heck, I can even exhort through text message if I'm short on time. What excuse do we really have? Especially when we know of its importance. Think about Solee. If her friend had said only once or twice in the beginning, "You can do this, hang in there," Solee probably would have given up in weariness earlier. But her friend continued to cheer her on, to the point where her words were helping to keep Solanna's little legs up. If Solee needed constant exhortation to hold on in a piddly volleyball practice, what kind of encouragement do you think we need to persevere through the deceitfulness of sin?

Christians should not be Sunday cheerleaders only. Why? Because we share in Christ, the one who held on through torture and ridicule. In our earlier Philippians verse, Paul said that it has been granted to us not only to believe in Christ, but to suffer for his sake (1:29). We may affirm that faith is a gift of grace, but suffering too? Later I will touch on how Hebrews 11 is full of those whose confession of hope resulted in life from death. They all suffered to the glory of God. And the beginning verses in Hebrews 12 bring us to the climax, Jesus Christ, who has received the promises as the author and finisher of our faith. The NKJV translates the beginning of Heb. 3:14, "For we have become partakers of Christ." Those in Christ share in all his benefits, so we can be confident that we will receive the promise. But it is also a gift of his grace that we share in his suffering. As he preserves us along the way, sanctifying us to his likeness, he gives us fellowship with one another to help us hold fast.

## AND YET AGAIN

As Hebrews 12:1–2 compares the Christian life of perseverance to a race, Hebrews 12:12 gives a picture of the weariness and despair that we all encounter through different obstacles in the run. In chapter 4, I will elaborate on the command this verse gives to lift up our drooping hands and strengthen our weak knees. But for now, notice how again in the verses immediately following we see this theological fitness illustration connected to an exhortation to the body of Christ.

> Strive for peace with everyone, and for the holiness without which no one will see the Lord. See to it that no one fails to obtain the grace of God; that no "root of bitterness" springs up and causes trouble, and by it many become defiled; that

no one is sexually immoral or unholy like Esau, who sold his birthright for a single meal. (12:14–16)

If you're like me, you might be thinking that it is awfully hard to reach peace when we're told to get this involved in everyone's personal business. But in order to really strive for peace, we need to be honestly examining both our fellow believers and ourselves. This is hard, because our motives have to be pure. First of all, since sin is so deceitful, as are our own hearts (Jer. 17:9), it can be extremely difficult to have an honest evaluation of our own condition. As we strive to do this in light of God's revealed Word and with the aid of his Spirit, we also need to depend on one another in love. And as we lovingly confront a fellow believer, it should be with a motive to restoration so that he or she, too, will obtain the grace of God. The preacher is calling the church to the hard task of redemptive engagement for the purity of the church and the glory of God.

While we aren't getting into particular sins here, you can see it isn't pretty. It is horrifying to see in ourselves, and it is very uncomfortable to approach those we care about who are falling away. Too often, we reason with ourselves that confrontation is more trouble than it's worth. And church discipline? Does anyone do that anymore? The answer is yes, if we care about the glory of God, the purity of the church, and the restoration of that person to the Lord. Perhaps it would be easier to be more open with one another if we were more concerned with what God promises than with what other people think.

The fact is that life is ugly sometimes. We get ourselves dirty when we shouldn't, and yet we need to get our hands dirty as we take on one another's burdens. We are exhorted to lift up our own drooping hands as well as to pick one another up. That is exactly what my brother's Tough Mudder team had to do to make it to the end.

But we know there are much harder obstacles in the Christian "race" than greasy quarter-pipes and electric shocks. Part of the grace and strength God gives us on our pilgrimage is the amazing camaraderie of our fellow pilgrims. As I watched the video clips of Luke's "Team Clinch" going through the Electroshock Therapy, I noticed that they formed a chain, everyone's hands resting on the shoulders of the person in front. It was a powerful image. To make it up the quarter-pipe wall, they formed another sort of chain, standing on one another's shoulders all the way to the top. At the crest were the strongest participants, encouraging as they pulled the next one over. Faith in action.

And they finished strong. They finished cold, muddy, bruised, tired, and glorious. They were awarded with the official Tough Mudder badge. I couldn't help but agree with the website's philosophy. The participants accomplished more than a physical feat; rather, they were a part of something that is experienced all too rarely these days. Has this been the Christian experience for you?

## GOING THE EXTRA MILE

1. My previous church was actually named Pilgrim Presbyterian, which is a great reminder of my pilgrim status. What exactly is a pilgrim? How does this status make us different from the rest of the world?

2. In Philippians 1:27 Paul tells us to stand firm in one spirit, with one mind. How does this exhortation play out when we are in disagreement over doctrine or practice? How important is theology to our Christian union?

3. The imagery of an advancing line of legionnaires against the enemy is both bold and intimate. Do you have relationships in your church that foster the vulnerability, trust, and soldiering that this illustration represents? When you are with your Christian brothers and sisters, do you have this

kind of selfless solidarity, or are you more concerned with how you've been offended by something or someone who's not measuring up?

4. Have you made a fighting effort to get to know Christ's bride?

5. How does the worship service affect your ideas about what is ordinary and what is extraordinary? Is ordinary bad? Why do you think God has ordained such ordinary means to convey such extraordinary grace?

6. Do you find that your involvement in technology has made it harder for you to pay attention? What are you sacrificing for the constant interruptions from media devices throughout the week? How does this compare to your willingness to be interrupted by the gospel?

7. Is regular church attendance important to you? How about membership?

8. When was the last time you were encouraged to persevere? What difference did it make?

# | 2 |

# IT DEPENDS ON HOW
# YOU READ THE SCALE

Now that we have established that we hold fast to our confession in the covenant community of the church, let's get into the nitty-gritty about our common goal and the way we relate to one another. Scripture uses the metaphor of a race to illustrate the church persevering in theological fitness, and I have added the modern-day twist of the Tough Mudder obstacles to keep it real. Now I would like to discuss the growth that is happening as we run together for the prize.

I have a goal: I want to be strong when I'm fifty. And I'm talking about muscles. Did you know that your muscles begin to deteriorate when you hit the big 5-0? I want a good head start so that I can keep my strength going as long as possible.

So I work out. And I happen to really like it.

Usually, most of my workouts include weights. Don't confuse this with body-builder weightlifting; it's more like eight- to ten-pound dumbbells in circuit training. But lately I've been really busy. I mean, busier than my normal crazy-busy. So I altered my workout routine a little to fit my schedule. Generally, I don't count most outdoor activity as my official workout because it's not all that intense. A bike ride with the kids, a walk with my husband, or bumping a volleyball with my girls are the bonuses that physical fitness frees me to do. These bonuses are actually the purpose for my goal of strength as I age. I want to contribute as much as I can to my physical fitness so that I can have an active life.

And yet, getting outside relieves stress. I needed some more sunshine and fresh air in my day. So I busted out the Rollerblades my husband bought me when I was about twenty-one years old. Usually when this happens, every kid in the neighborhood gets excited, grabbing whatever Big Wheel, bike, or mode of transportation they can find, and following me as if I'm the Pied Piper. I wouldn't call it much of a workout. But this time I took it up a notch and they weren't as excited to hang with me. I thought I'd actually start to incorporate rollerblading into my workout routine. I go fast enough for the neighbors to think I'm weird for about forty minutes. It has been such a great change-up that I happily enjoy this workout two to three times a week.

However, I had a sneaking suspicion. I'm not one to jump on the scale constantly, but after about three weeks of this I wondered what less-intense, fewer-weight workouts read on the scale. Sure enough, I had lost weight. Usually, a girl would be happy with this news. But I knew why. It wasn't because I had resisted the German chocolate cake and cookies. It wasn't because I was burning crazy-mad calories rollerblading either. I wasn't noticeably any thinner. I had probably lost muscle.

It isn't horrible, I know. But I hate to settle. After all, I have a goal. This really got me thinking about how one may look ostensibly, regardless of what's really going on inside. It also got me thinking about how focused one needs to be to keep one's muscles strong.

You see the spiritual analogy here, I'm sure. The apostle Paul used the comparison of racing as an exhortation to both determination and discipline.

> Do you not know that in a race all the runners run, but only one receives the prize? So run that you may obtain it. Every ath-

lete exercises self-control in all things. They do it to receive a perishable wreath, but we an imperishable. So I do not run aimlessly; I do not box as one beating the air. But I discipline my body and keep it under control, lest after preaching to others I myself should be disqualified. (1 Cor. 9:24–27)

Paul is illustrating that perseverance requires focus on a singular goal. Our goal as Christians is our glorification, to reign with Christ in the new heavens and the new earth in righteousness. It takes faithful pursuit to continue toward our goal without being distracted. And keeping focused on our objective helps us to put everything else into perspective.

## SINGLE-MINDED ON AN UNSEEN GOAL

My personal goal for physical strength is about perseverance. Studies show that seventy-year-olds who athletically train still have great muscles. Yes, there is still deterioration with age, but the aging muscles of the physically fit are pretty impressive. This aids in their all-around physical health. The unseen muscle tissue does color the overall way that one feels in everyday life. It affects performance and sustains health. Likewise, there is much unseen going on in our spiritual lives. Both physical perseverance and spiritual perseverance require fight. In our spiritual perseverance, we are fighting for holiness. And just as with strong muscles, holy living liberates the members of the body of Christ to better serve one another and enjoy his blessings.

What are our primary goals for spiritual growth? Paul is warning the believer against presumption and is highlighting the discipline involved in growth. You may think that I am a little over the top or single-minded in my physical goal. But isn't that how Paul is exhorting us to be in our spiritual lives as well? Earlier in this same letter he states that he's determined to know nothing among them other than Jesus Christ and him crucified (1 Cor. 2:2).

Do you strive for that singular goal? What will this mean for your own self-interests when they are weighing you down for finishing the race? You have to have a goal to persevere. This goal determines how you read the scale. But it isn't as easy as it may sound to be so singularly focused. We can't look to ourselves for this kind of hard work. The strength of our faith is in God's faithfulness, and he is the one perfecting us for holiness. That is why our focus is singular. And Paul encourages us,

> So we do not lose heart. Though our outer self is wasting away, our inner self is being renewed day by day. For this light momentary affliction is preparing for us an eternal weight of glory beyond all comparison, as we look not to the things that are seen but to the things that are unseen. For the things that are seen are transient, but the things that are unseen are eternal. (2 Cor. 4:16–18)

No matter how hard we physically train, our bodies are still perishing. But the eternal weight of glory is awaiting us. God is glorified in all our weakness, for it is his strength that we count on. His strength never deteriorates. And so we can look forward to that new, imperishable body that we will be able to worship him in for eternity. This lofty goal enables us to persevere in our Christian lives as well as in taking care of the body he has entrusted us with in the meantime.

## HOW MANY PEOPLE CAN HOP ON ONE SCALE?

Sometimes I find myself noticing another strong person, and a whole host of unhealthy questions fill my mind. I wonder how tall she is, how much she weighs, and what size pants she wears. Really, I do. Then I compare my imaginary answers to my own statistics. If that person looks healthy, fit, and strong, I wonder how I measure up. Just like that, I lose my focus. Pride creeps in. I want to be stronger, more fit, and healthier than this person who has hampered my self-image. This is what happens when we begin comparing ourselves with others. We lose our focus and fall into sin.

Who cares about my self-image? Let's face it—we all have an unhealthy self-image. This is just a term that we use to evaluate how we think we stand compared to others. We either inflate our self-image in arrogance or feel sorry for ourselves that we are not good enough. When it comes to weight, self-image has to shut up when we step on the scale. Actual numbers appear, forcing us into reality. The numbers are numbers. And yet we can use these numbers to play the comparison game, inviting our self-image back into our convoluted assessments. We know that it is silly. After all, people come in many different body types. A healthy weight for me is likely to be a good bit different from the ideal weight of my best friend.

The problem with self-image is the self. I don't want such a narcissistic focus. And when I play the comparison game, I am drawing others into my narcissism while I try to ascertain where "I" measure up. All of a sudden, "me and the scale" becomes me against every healthy woman in my sights.

This physical comparing is certainly indicative of what I can also get caught up doing in my spiritual life. I have a sanctification self-image problem as well. Do you ever size up someone else's spiritual maturity and compare it to your own? How ugly is that? And just like our physical self-image, our spiritual assessments of others and ourselves can be very convoluted. We can't measure our own sanctification when we are focused on ourselves. Sanctification isn't only about what we may look like on the outside as compared to everyone else. Thinking this way just leads to faking it. And let me tell you, you cannot fake it to the end of the race and receive a crown.

And yet there is a recognizable fruit that gets noticed as we grow in holiness. Jesus said that we will know one another by our fruits (see Matt. 7:15–23). As you know, fruit doesn't grow when the roots are no good and the plant isn't properly nourished and maintained. The fruits of holiness are signs of an inner working. Thankfully, we do have Someone to compare ourselves to, Someone who is perfectly holy. If our focus is on Christ, then we will be directed to his living Word that provides all we need to know him and live a holy life (2 Tim. 3:16–17).

And since believers are united to Christ, we have a new relationship with the scale of holiness. The law is no longer our enemy that condemns us, but our friend that guides us to holiness with the power of the Spirit.

## THE GOOD, THE BAD, AND THE . . . BEAUTIFUL

Of course, this process isn't clean and pretty. All Christians are tempted to sin, all the time. And this is so frustrating! We are ashamed of our sin as we fight to mortify it and strive for holiness. So what do good Christians do when they have a broken heart or a hurtful disagreement, don't get that job they're after, or are just exhausted with life? Do we just pretend that we aren't tempted to sin? Do we hide our struggles and try to look like good, healthy Christians? What does a good, healthy Christian look like?

God is faithful to his covenant, and he is much more concerned with the reality of our broken hearts than with how we look through the process. And he will humble us to reveal the sinful attitudes and actions that we think we have so carefully hidden. We need to know that he is sufficient in all our afflictions. In this area of trust, we need theological fitness, mental fitness, and even emotional fitness.

If you think about it, we are all crazy. Sin is crazy. Wanting to be fulfilled by anything other than Jesus Christ is crazy! Looking to anything else for meaning and value is just plain nuts. We need to acknowledge our own craziness so that we see our need for Christ. This means being honest about the ugliness of our sin. But if we're too busy hiding our sin and acting like sanctified Christians, we are really on a self-atonement plan that is the craziest idea of all!

While there may be no scale to help us measure our Christian fitness levels, God does give us his living Word to expose the condition of our hearts. The preacher to the Hebrews reminds his readers how God's Word at Sinai actually uncovered the lack of faith of a whole generation. They failed to reach their rest because of their faithlessness. And we are exhorted,

> Let us therefore strive to enter that rest, so that no one may fall by the same sort of disobedience. For the word of God is living and active, sharper than any two-edged sword, piercing to the division of soul and spirit, of joints and of marrow, and discerning the thoughts and intentions of the heart. And no creature is hidden from his sight, but all are naked and exposed to the eyes of him to whom we must give account. (Heb. 4:11–13)

God gives us a lot more than numbers. His Word works like a scalpel,[1] revealing the devastation of our sin while also offering a blessed, holy Savior. Although our own discriminating abilities may be depraved, God's Word is perceptive and penetrating to every part of our being. He reveals our true condition, which is in utter despair apart from him. Sometimes honestly examining ourselves in light of God's Word can feel as painful as it would to be cut with a scalpel. I think this is part of the beautiful process of sanctification—an increased understanding of our own helplessness apart from Jesus Christ. This is what we are striving for, a rest that we can find only in God's Son. When he is set before us, there is nothing to compare.

1. David L. Allen describes how the term used for *sword* may convey the meaning of a surgeon's knife, which contributes to the linguistic argument for the authorship of Luke in Hebrews. See David L. Allen, *Lukan Authorship of Hebrews* (Nashville: B&H, 2010), 94. Disclaimer: I am not affirming that Luke is the writer of Hebrews (though we can all agree that the Holy Spirit is the author), but this book does the scholarly work to make Luke a contender.

This is also our encouragement. Because we are made righteous in Jesus Christ, we are new creations called to live a life of faith and obedience. Paul lays it out plain for us in Romans (see esp. Romans 6) when he asserts that believers have died to sin, so how can we live in it? Just as a married person has a new status, so does a Christian. After the moment I said the words "I do," I was no longer single. Because of my new status, I needed to live as a wife, not as a single woman. Likewise, Paul explains that since we were united to Christ in his death, we are all the more united in his resurrection. Therefore we no longer have the pedigree of that "old self" who was enslaved to sin. We are new creations under the reign of grace! Sin no longer reigns in us, and knowing this new status changes everything.

We are not fighting to improve our old selves, but we are striving to live as new creations in Christ. This means that we enjoy the benefits of our union with him. As Jesus is at the right hand of his Father this very moment interceding on behalf of his people as our Great High Priest, his Holy Spirit is applying Christ's work to us and helping us along the way. Therefore, we are "slaves to righteousness," as Paul puts it. The fruit produced from our sin was rotten indeed.

> But now that you have been set free from sin and have become slaves of God, the fruit you get leads to sanctification and its end, eternal life. For the wages of sin is death, but the free gift of God is eternal life in Christ Jesus our Lord. (Rom. 6:22–23)

## DO I SIN LESS NOW?

This leads to another question. If we really are growing in the faith, shouldn't we be sinning less? What does it mean to be a mature Christian? After all, since we are being sanctified and transformed into Christ's likeness, I would expect that at thirty-seven I would not be struggling with sin like I was at seventeen. Well, I have a yes and a no to this answer.

*Yes.* Looking back to my seventeen-year-old self certainly makes me feel holier. Many of the sins that I committed on a regular basis back then are not even desirable to me anymore. For that I am very thankful. And in the twenty years that have passed, God has given me better desires. I get upset with myself now because I find my desires to be too small. But compared to Aimee at seventeen, they are much deeper. I see the fruit of righteousness being cultivated in my life.

I am truly amazed by God's grace in saving me from my seventeen-year-old self! When I think back to the end of high school and the beginning of college, it is astonishing that I am even alive. I indulged in many sins that one would expect a teenager-who-thinks-she's-an-adult to commit. I was immature, and in many ways I was expected to be immature. I cavalierly took advantage of these expectations, as well as the grace of God. I knew I was behaving like a lost person even though I belonged to Christ. The ways that God has matured me have surely exceeded my expectations at seventeen. And yet my barometer of holiness is not to be compared to a younger version of myself; it is to be compared to the holy God.

*No.* Here I am at thirty-seven, torn up over my sin on a regular basis. If God has been faithful in my sanctification, why am I still struggling so much with my sin? As you probably know from experience yourself, in his grace God progressively reveals our sin to us as we grow in holiness. It's not so much that we're developing new sins as Christians; rather it's that our sins have been developing, and now God is going to reveal them to us as he prepares us to face them. As we grow in our love for the Lord, we also hate our sin more. As we meditate on the cross, we are exposed. Here's how Milton Vincent explains it:

> The deeper I go into the gospel, the more I comprehend and confess aloud the depth of my sinfulness. A gruesome death like

the one that Christ endured for me would only be required for one who is exceedingly sinful and unable to appease a holy God. Consequently, whenever I consider the necessity and manner of His death, along with the love and selflessness behind it, I am laid bare and utterly exposed for the sinner I am.[2]

With growth comes a mature awareness of our sin. I would like to think that I am sinning less as a thirty-seven-year-old, but a growing understanding of the severe depth of my sinfulness also assures me of the processes of sanctification. At seventeen, I was well aware of a list of sins that I was committing. I even knew that some of them were pretty bad. But I had the immature idea that as I grew, I would knock off those sins one by one and then be a mature Christian. I was completely deceived about the gravity of my sinfulness.

Repentance has become much more dear to me as I have grown in holiness. Because of Jesus' death and resurrection, we can know that we are no longer dead in our sins but alive in Christ (Eph. 2:1, 5). Because we are forgiven and have the work of his Spirit applying Christ's accomplishment on our behalf, we can push forward toward holiness. Our unity in Christ gives us a growing longing and desire to know him and be like him.

And because of our union with Christ, we truly are being sanctified. Only God knows the number of our sins, but every one of them was paid for by Christ's blood. Yes, we are saved by grace, but that grace is expensive. Therefore we abhor sin, hold fast to God's promises in Christ, and, by his Spirit, we are now able to mortify sin and truly grow toward our assured goal of glorification with him. "And I am sure of this, that he who began a good work in you will bring it to completion at the day of Jesus Christ" (Phil. 1:6).

2. Milton Vincent, *A Gospel Primer for Christians: Learning to See the Glories of God's Love* (Bemidji, MN: Focus Publishing, 2008), 33.

## BECOMING LIKE CHRIST

So often we understand how we are justified by grace, but then we rely on our own self-righteousness to try and sanctify ourselves. After all, we are to strive for holiness, working out our own salvation with fear and trembling (Phil. 2:12). We know that sanctification involves an active faith in good works, and we want to do well. But what is the basis and source for our deeds? How do we know whether we are truly maturing in Christ? Mark Jones explains the relationship between impetration and application when it comes to our sanctification.

> Impetration—not a concept that is well known to readers today—has in view Christ's meritorious work; application refers to the enjoyment of Christ's purchase of redemption. The two concepts are distinct but not separate. So to be holy is both to look to Christ's work of reconciliation (i.e. impetration) and to labor after conformity to his image (Eph. 1:4; Rom. 8:29).[3]

Our hope is to be like Christ, nothing less. And Jones reminds us that Jesus Christ, as the God-man, also had to live by faith. "Because Christ is the holiest man ever to have lived, he is the greatest believer ever to have lived (Heb. 12:2). There has never been, nor will there ever be, a more perfect example of living by faith than Jesus."[4] In my sanctification, I look to Christ's person and his work.

> By faith, he believed the word and promises of God. Furthermore, Christ did not merely exercise faith for himself; he also exercised faith for all those for whom he died, so that they may receive from him that particular grace. For there is no

3. Mark Jones, *Antinomianism: Reformed Theology's Unwelcome Guest?* (Phillipsburg, NJ: P&R, 2013), 22.
4. Ibid., 23.

grace we receive that was not first present in Christ himself, particularly the grace of faith. As Richard Sibbes notes, "We must know that all things are first in Christ, and then in us."

The life of holiness is therefore the life of faith. The way we begin the Christian life is the way we continue in the Christian life until we get to heaven, where faith becomes sight.[5]

The great gift of faith doesn't stop at our justification, but it causes us to continue to trust in God to sanctify us as we press on. That same faith that looked to Christ for a declaration of holiness now looks to him for the strength and ability to live in holiness. Surely, sanctification is no passive process; it is a daily struggle. But the struggle is part of the blessing. Christians deplore sin and love God's law. We are no longer under the reign of sin but the reign of grace (Rom. 5:21). And since we are given his Spirit, we can strive to obey God's Word with confidence, knowing that our efforts are blessed in Christ.

## WORKING IT OUT

Exhortations in Scripture such as "Work out your own salvation with fear and trembling" (Phil. 2:12) are weighty. But as I was just reminded when listening to Derek Thomas expound this verse,[6] we are told to "work *out*" our salvation, not "work *for*" it. This takes exercising our faith in everyday living. We don't just confess our faith together on Sunday morning and then move about the week unchanged. We hold fast to our confession of hope that we are chosen in Christ and set apart for God, and that shapes our lives. As we read in Hebrews,

> For he who sanctifies and those who are sanctified all have one source. This is why he is not ashamed to call them brothers, saying,

---

5. Ibid. The Richard Sibbes quote is from *The Works of the Reverend Richard Sibbes* (Aberdeen: J. Chalmers, 1809), 1:103.

6. Derek Thomas, "The Holy Christian Life" (lecture, Proclamation Presbyterian Church, Philadelphia, PA, May 3, 2014).

A gift from
# John Paul Baker

*Hi Don and Laura, Something more
for you to read and think over.
From John Paul Baker*

> "I will tell of your name to my brothers;
> in the midst of the congregation I will sing your praise."

And again,

> "I will put my trust in him."

And again,

> "Behold, I and the children God has given me." (Heb. 2:11–13)

Arthur Pink points out how these verses highlight that it is "in Christ that we were chosen, and from Christ that we receive the Spirit, and as it is by the constant application of Christ's work and the constant communication of His life that we live and grow, Christ is our sanctification."[7] Like I've said, our theology shapes the way we live. As I learn that Christ is my sanctification, I have a growing desire to live as one who is set apart for God. This group of quotations taken from the Psalms and Isaiah show us a Savior who proclaims his glorious Father to us, who lived with perfect faith, and who identifies himself with all those whom God has given him. As we strive to live the Christian life of faith and obedience, our sanctification is secured by the work of the One who went before us and who is now at the right hand of the Father, interceding on our behalf. By faith, we look to the One whose sacrifice

> has brought us into the presence of God. By the Word, by God's truth, by the indwelling Spirit, He continually sanctifies his believers. He gave himself for the church 'that he might sanctify and cleanse it by the washing of water by the Word' (Eph. 5:26)....
> Christ himself is the foundation, source, method, and channel of our sanctification. . . . In what other way are we sanctified

7. Arthur W. Pink, *An Exposition of Hebrews* (Grand Rapids: Baker, 2004), 120.

day by day, but by taking hold of the salvation which is by Him, "The Lamb that is slain"?[8]

He is the beginning and the end, but he is also the middle. He is the one we fight for and the one who fights with us. He is our power to fight and our example to follow. When our eyes are on Christ, when we hold fast to the truth of his promise, we want to be obedient, we despise our own sin, and we fight to persevere to the end.

Stepping on the scale takes vulnerability. So does looking at the condition of our own hearts. But when we hold the gospel before us every day, we can live honestly, confessing our sins, because we know we are in the hands of a mighty and compassionate Savior. The fight to persevere isn't always pretty. But we have a Savior who has covered our shame with his own blood, has clothed us in a robe of righteousness, and intercedes on our behalf even now.

## HOW DO YOU READ THE SCALE?

God's scale of judgment has no curve. He doesn't seek out whomever came the closest to a righteous life and lower his standards of holiness to the level they reached. Just because I may seem more spiritually mature than my struggling neighbor, Betty, it doesn't mean that I have made myself more deserving of God's grace. This way of thinking is contradictory to grace. And, trust me, we don't want what we really deserve. We are saved by grace alone, through faith alone, in Christ alone, to the glory of God alone.[9] God's standard is 100 percent righteousness, and Jesus Christ has fulfilled all righteousness. Along with his righteous offering, our Savior

8. Ibid.
9. These are four of the five "solas" of the Reformation: "Sola Gratia" (Grace Alone); "Sola Fide" (Faith Alone); "Solus Christus" (Christ Alone); and "Soli Deo Gloria" (To God Alone Be Glory).

also took our place in receiving the just punishment for our sin. And so in Hebrews we learn that in Christ we are no longer under the old covenant of the law, which we could not fulfill. "But as it is, Christ has obtained a ministry that is as much more excellent than the old as the covenant he mediates is better, since it is enacted on better promises" (8:6).[10] Jesus is our blessed Mediator.

We wrongly want to keep a tally of our own comparative score in the Christian life, but our fictional numbers do not equal accomplishment. Dave Harvey encourages us to be ambitious for the right thing.

> God's glorious agenda for our ambition, like his glorious gospel, begins not with what we achieve but *who we are*.
>
> Walking in a manner worthy of the calling to which we've been called means I have a new ambition. Instead of gunning for my own glory or comfort, I'm ambitious for a changed life.[11]

What reward are we really after? Whom are we trying to please? These questions reveal our hearts and shape our pursuit. Are we after God's glory, or our own? As we seek God's glory, we don't measure our own so-called accomplishments, because our reward is far greater than we can ever attain on our own. It is Christ himself, and we will not rest until we see him face to face.

## GOING THE EXTRA MILE

1. You have to have a goal to persevere. This goal determines how you read the scale. We learn from 2 Corinthians 4:16–18 that the Christian goal is unseen. How does this affect the way that we press on? What difficulties does it bring?

10. I will teach more about these covenants in chapter 9.
11. Dave Harvey, *Rescuing Ambition* (Wheaton, IL: Crossway, 2010), 67.

2. Why is self-image really a hoax? How might this change the way that we comfort and counsel others?

3. What ideas that you hold about how sanctification "looks" might need to be challenged in light of this chapter? How might that affect the way you look at your fellow believers "in the race"?

4. How have you changed throughout your Christian walk? As you grow in holiness, how have your ideas about the extent of your own sinfulness been challenged?

5. How do we know if we are really maturing in Christ?

6. Do you agree that the fight to persevere doesn't always look pretty? If so, how can we be more honest about how God is working in our lives? Why do we feel so compelled to candy-coat our spiritual condition?

7. Sometimes we can conjure up our own imaginary scale with our so-called "Christian scorecard." Paul tells us in Philippians 3:4–7 that he held an impeccable score by all outward signs. And yet he counted it all as dung (v. 8 KJV). What did he trade it for? How did he estimate the real value of his works? How does this encourage you as a Christian?

# PART 2

# "HOLD FAST"

| 3 |

# SUPERABUNDANTLY ENGAGED

I remember well the first time the teacher in my childbirth classes introduced coping techniques for pain. Everyone received a Ziploc bag of ice. We were instructed to clench tightly to this ice for sixty seconds, all the while doing our "special breathing." No one could last. It was painful! And instead of distracting us from the pain, the breathing just felt like an annoying add-on. The pain was much more bothersome than anticipated, and I saw no value in completing this task. It was just ice.

This also provoked a very scary thought. As the popular hymn goes, there was no turning back. There was a real life growing inside of me, and it was going to come out. It *had* to come out. I was going to have to go through with this long, torturous labor, and I couldn't even hold on to a bag of ice for sixty seconds! What was I thinking? As my pregnancy progressed I developed conspiracy theories, because there was no way that baby was really going to come out. I began looking at all mothers suspiciously. They knew something I didn't, some secret about the way that babies were born. There had to be some kind of privileged information that isn't revealed until it's "go" time.

Thankfully, I was able to make it through three labors and deliveries and to meet my goal of coping through the pain without drug use. Sure, I found the breathing techniques to be more helpful in this real situation, but there was definitely a motivating difference that helped me to persevere. I wasn't holding on to a bag of ice; I was holding on to the truth that I (hopefully) wasn't going to die, and that I would have a beautiful baby in the end. Now, by no means am I trying to make you think I was a model student in the labor and delivery room. Let's just say that everyone in that room (and perhaps the hallway) was well aware of my suffering. But I held on.

In our Hebrews 10:23 verse, we are exhorted to hold fast the confession of our hope. We have established that we are not left to do this alone, but are to encourage one another with the good news of the gospel in the covenant community of the church. We also touched on our common goal and how we all look different in the process of sanctification. But maybe this appeal to hold fast sounds a bit vague to you. What does it really mean? And how do you do it—in real life? I propose that this is both very simple and extremely difficult.

Put simply, holding fast means that you grab tightly and don't let go. But I think that my labor and delivery teacher made a very good point. You have to be prepared to deal with suffering. Endurance takes stamina. Stamina takes training.

Faith is a fighting grace. Do not mistake it for an easy believism or a passive coast until the roll is called up yonder. Having a confession is not enough. We must hold fast to it. And so we fight to hold fast to our hope no matter what. The beginning of Hebrews 12 shows us that we must persevere in holiness to reach the crown at the end of the race. In case you think I am making too much out of this whole idea of holding on, let me show you some other references that connect perseverance to holding fast (starting with Hebrews):

> For we have come to share in Christ, if indeed we *hold* our original confidence firm to the end. (Heb. 3:14)

Since then we have a great high priest who has passed through the heavens, Jesus, the Son of God, let us *hold fast* our confession. (Heb. 4:14)

So when God desired to show more convincingly to the heirs of the promise the unchangeable character of his purpose, he guaranteed it with an oath, so that by two unchangeable things, in which it is impossible for God to lie, we who have fled for refuge might have strong encouragement to *hold fast* to the hope set before us. (Heb. 6:17, 18)

Let us *hold fast* the confession of our hope without wavering, for he who promised is faithful. (Heb. 10:23)

Now I would remind you, brothers, of the gospel I preached to you, which you received, in which you stand, and by which you are being saved, if you *hold fast* to the word I preached to you—unless you believed in vain. (1 Cor. 15:1–2)

Do all things without grumbling or questioning . . . *holding fast* to the word of life, so that in the day of Christ I may be proud that I did not run in vain or labor in vain. (Phil. 2:14, 16)

Do not despise prophecies, but test everything; *hold fast* what is good. (1 Thess. 5:20–21)

Only *hold fast* what you have until I come. The one who conquers and who keeps my works until the end, to him I will give authority over the nations. (Rev. 2:25, 26)

We see that this exhortation to hold fast requires a *theological* fitness because we are required to lay hold of the gospel. It is one thing to say that I am a Christian and to make a profession of faith. But it takes a level of skill and practice in what we are confessing to hold fast to it.[1] When the gospel is revealed to us, we receive it by faith, we are qualified for the Christian life, and then we are privileged to learn more and more about what it means and how we are to live accordingly. As we are trained from God's Word and put our faith to practice by the power of his Spirit, our competency and stamina increase. Our own fitness levels develop from a *persistent fight to exercise our faith by actively engaging in the gospel truth revealed in God's Word*. It's fairly easy to say that we believe something, but it is much more difficult "to continue in and press forward along the path we profess to have entered; and that, not with-standing all the threats of persecutors, sophistical reasonings of false teachers, and allurements of the world."[2] To persevere in the truth we profess, we are told to hold tight to our confession through it all.

Thomas Schreiner puts it well: "Perseverance, then, is noth-ing other than grasping the scandal of the cross until the day we die."[3] It's that simple. We tend to associate perseverance with our own righteousness to prove our holiness. But we will utterly fail if we hold on to our own bare works. "The author [of Hebrews] does not commend perfection to his readers. Rather, he exhorts them to continue to hold on to Jesus Christ, to continue to cling to his sacrifice for forgiveness of sins. . . . Believers persevere by continuing to find their forgiveness and final sanctification in Christ instead of themselves."[4] This knowledge and trust in Christ liberates us to strive for holiness to the end because we know that he is blessing our efforts, whatever flaws they may have. Christ's righteousness proves our holiness. Believers have been sealed with his Holy Spirit applying his work to us. And

1. See Arthur W. Pink, *An Exposition of Hebrews* (Grand Rapids: Baker, 2004), 597.
2. Ibid.
3. Thomas R. Schreiner, *Run to Win the Prize: Perseverance in the New Testament* (Wheaton, IL: Crossway, 2010), 76.
4. Ibid., 80.

so we trust that he is working in us as we hold fast to living a holy life.

This is a relief! And yet, as wonderful as it is that we hold on to God's promises in Christ, we find ourselves in a great struggle not to let go. Did you catch those last two words? Perseverance is not about "letting go." It is not passive. Sure, we will discuss later the command to lay aside the weights and sin that hold us back (Heb. 12:1), but even this is active. And it is done with the positive focus of holding fast to the truth. I think we need to take this back to the training mats.

## TRAINING

About four years ago, I decided it was time to get more seriously involved in a workout routine. Having been raised in a family that values physical fitness, I have always lived a somewhat active life. However, in my thirties it became apparent that my body was not as obliging to my requests. It was time to get a little more disciplined if I wanted to feel as strong as I did in my twenties. So I did the practical thing for a mother of three: I started buying DVD workouts by experienced trainers. The first workout I did was an hour long. As I was chugging along I thought to myself, "You're a little winded, Aimee, but you've still got it!"

And then I woke up the next morning. Whoever thought it would hurt so much to go *down* stairs? And bending—what an arduous task when your muscles are screaming at you! The morning-after soreness just told me I needed strengthening, I wasn't in my twenties anymore, and the exercise was working. So, even in pain, I kept at it six days a week.

The Christian life is littered with obstacles. Athletes train for these kinds of things. Have you ever known a professional athlete who trained alone or without a plan? While I might be able to think of some good exercises, I do not have the knowledge to put together the most beneficial workout routine. And I certainly wouldn't go for a full hour unless I was being led. Many of the workouts I do combine circuit training and super-sets. I surely wouldn't have thought of concepts such as combining emphasis on aerobic and anaerobic metabolic systems or active rest on my own. But these trainers have a plan for me to follow.

Often, the routines require each circuit to be repeated. There are many benefits to this. The first time through, my muscles and my brain are being introduced to the form. However, the second time around is even more advantageous. Now I already know the technique. So if I'm told it's time for the second set of UFCs or sissy squats, I know what in the world that means as well as the technique involved. At this point my muscles are reaching fatigue, and I am told this is good because that is where "the magic happens." Muscles are being further toned the second time through. This point of muscle fatigue is also the point in the workout when I ask, "Why did I get myself into this?" That's when I know change is happening.

Where am I going with all this? Much of our conditioning in the Christian life is hard. As biblical pastors, teachers, and mentors lead us, we realize that we aren't quite as spiritually fit as we thought we were. When we face a challenge or obstacle, we find that our strength and stamina are weak. First we have to learn the form. Theology has specialized language just like every other discipline. For my workouts, I need to learn lingo such as *skull crushers*, *spider push-ups*, and *supination arm extensions*. When we learn what the Bible teaches about God's redemptive plan through Jesus Christ, there's all kinds of vocabulary involved such as *propitiation*, *imputation*, *eschatology*, and *covenant*. Also, in many of our first experiences in trying to live in light of the gospel, we fall on our faces. We are in a continuous battle with sin. But through repentance and prayer, the Lord uses even those times to strengthen us. When we encounter our new vocabulary the second time, we know it and can learn more deeply by the use of it. When we encounter a similar temptation again, we are stronger and wiser to turn away. Our trust in the Lord grows as we see how he has been faithful all along.

There will be many blessings throughout our Christian lives. But there will also be times when we ask ourselves how we got into all this. And, sure, there are obvious moments in life when this question is our wisdom talking, telling us we shouldn't be involved in a particular situation. It is a discerning question. Many times this question comes because we did not properly count the cost. It demands of us that we estimate the value and purpose of our cause. But make no mistake, we will find that the most valuable things in life bring us to fatigue. That's when we are toning—during the "burn."

## PAY ATTENTION!

The key to holding fast is focus. The sermon-letter to the Hebrews has a forward-looking focus. The preacher keeps reminding the reader where Christ is *now*. When we get to the section on the details of our confession, we will be looking at Psalm 110. Here we see that Jesus is sitting at the right hand of the Father, ruling and interceding on our behalf. While emphasizing that our Lord's redemptive work to justify his people is finished, the preacher to the Hebrews also points us to our future hope that awaits us at the end of the marathon. We see in Hebrews chapter 11 that the promise the Old Testament believers held fast to was not something that would be fulfilled before the resurrection. They were looking toward a better country (11:16), one that would never be shaken (12:27–28). We are running toward something, and we hold fast to this truth.

Sometimes I can talk my husband, Matt, into doing my workout videos with me. One of the trainers is constantly telling us to be "engaged." Matt and I have made a little joke out of it because he pronounces the word with a funny emphasis: *en-gayged*. The first syllable is higher pitched and the imaginary "y" is held an extra beat. We always repeat after him with our own impersonation. But the trainer is emphasizing the word to make a very important point. Doing the workout isn't just about going through the motions. The benefits are more substantial when we are engaged in the process.

This is a principle that I am trying to teach my children to apply when sitting under the preached Word. It's called *active listening*. Sit up, make eye contact, take some notes, and ask questions in your head while the sermon is being preached. Make connections to other areas of Scripture. Tie it in to your life experiences. Be engaged in the sermon. This is another area that requires mental fitness.

In other words, pay attention. That is exactly the exhortation that the preacher to the Hebrews gives in his very first warning to persevere. "Therefore we must pay much closer attention to what we have heard, lest we drift away from it" (Heb. 2:1). The preacher has already declared that God has spoken to us in these last days by his Son. He then makes a case that Jesus Christ is superior to even angels. If Jesus is better than the angels, then his message must be of greater significance as well. Following verse 1 we read, "For since the message declared by angels proved to be reliable, and every transgression or disobedience received a just retribution, how shall we escape if we neglect such a great salvation?" (2:2–3). Here we see this popular argument of the less to the greater. The angels had participated in delivering the law of Moses. The recipients of this sermon knew how crucial the law was. They were also aware of the sanctions for breaking the law. But both Moses and the angels worked for Jesus. The law could never save. So it is at great peril that one would neglect Christ's message of salvation through him. There is no confession of hope without Jesus.

Notice how similar this warning is to the exhortations to hold fast. The words are very similar in the Greek concordance.

For "hold fast," *katĕchō*,[5] we see words like "keep (in memory), possess, retain, seize on, and stay."[6] And for our phrase "pay attention," προσέχειν (*prosechein*), we see similar words "to hold to, tend to, turn to."[7] The King James Version translates "give the more earnest heed" where the English Standard uses "pay much closer attention." I like how this adverb for "earnest," *perissoteros*, also translates "more superabundantly."[8] My own housewife theologian translation (that's HWTV) is inspired to be *superabundantly engaged* in God's Word, intensely involved. Isn't that what holding fast really is?

As the Holy Spirit opens our hearts to the promises of God, he also gives us a desire to learn from God's Word and walk in it. But we still need to exhort one another not to just go through the motions. Pay attention to the gem that we have, give heed to God's Word, and get engaged with its message of salvation. One key way to be engaged is through prayer. And again, we have the help of God's Holy Spirit as we are privileged to approach our Father in prayer. God doesn't use his angels as mediators to and from him in prayer, but uses his own Son, Jesus Christ. He is both the message and the means. If we neglect his message of salvation, how can we escape apostasy and judgment? How can we possibly approach the almighty God?

As sure as Jesus paid our ransom and won the victory for his kingdom on the cross, he will return to consummate that kingdom. We can be assured of this because he was resurrected and has now ascended to the right hand of the Father until all his enemies are made a footstool. Pay attention to what is to

---

5. My friend Todd Pruitt also pointed out that this is the word that we get *catechize* and *catechism* from, which is what we are aiming for when we teach the faith. We certainly want our children to "hold" to what we are teaching them.

6. James Strong, LLD, STD, *The New Strong's Exhaustive Concordance of the Bible* (Nashville: Thomas Nelson, 1990), Strong's number 2722.

7. See "Hebrews 2:1," Bible Hub, accessed March 6, 2015, http://biblelexicon.org/hebrews/2-1.htm.

8. Ibid.

come, and you will be encouraged to endure the trials on the way. Be superabundantly engaged in his promise and you will not turn away to anything else. As your focus is strengthened to the glory of God, your intensity to hold fast will strengthen. When faced with sin and adversity, you will find that perseverance to get back up again and stay the course.

## GET YOUR ARMS UP! A FIGHTING MENTALITY IN PERSEVERANCE

I used to think that my family was strange. There was a distinctive mentality I was raised in as a daughter of a martial arts teacher. Some families discuss current events over the dinner table and consider how they have contributed to society that day. My family would talk about how "Randy" trained until he puked. I loved to hear some of the classes my dad would put together. He was always thinking of ways to train for real-life self-defense. On one occasion he scattered chairs around the room and had two students spar, shirtless, holding markers. The markers represented knives, so there really was a visible "wound" to gauge. And the chairs were obstacles representing the fact that most people don't have the luxury of an open dojo when defending themselves.

Testing for belts was always exciting. Dad would integrate different exercises into the fitness training. For a while, they were doing some running at the beginning of class. Students were timed while they ran through the neighborhood. Testing was at least a week long, and it involved different categories such as fitness, writing a paper, sparring, and even old school forms. But you never knew what Dad was going to pull on test week. And you signed a waiver affirming this fearful truth. So when one student was going for his black belt, what he thought was going to be a normal fitness run turned into, "You have a ten-second head start before I let one of my best guys loose. If he catches up to you, be ready to fight." Oh, he didn't get caught; he ran the best time on his record.

That same poor student thought he was being tested on forms one evening. So did his unsuspecting parents who were there video recording. My dad asked him if he could record the student's answers while asking him some questions throughout the night. As Dad ostensibly went to push "record," he blasted Aerosmith, which was the signal for the two guys waiting upstairs to run down with a blitz attack. Good times.

You might think that one would have to be a little crazy to participate in this kind of training. Probably. I wasn't anywhere near a dedicated student. But although I was in and out, and focused on way too many shallow activities in my youth, this strand of craziness still developed in me. My workout mentality now is to train hard, or what's the point? I'm disappointed in myself when I don't. If I'm in so much pain that it hurts to go down the stairs, I know I've trained well. With my busy lifestyle, I'm not involved in that kind of rigorous training very often. But I respect it. Occasionally I still like to talk about it at the dinner table.

This background, this strand of craziness if you will, is what helped me to have an even deeper understanding when it came time to teach my Bible study on Hebrews 12:12–13. In the context of perseverance and holding fast the confession of our hope, the writer of this sermon-letter exhorts the reader,

> Therefore lift your drooping hands and strengthen your weak knees, and make straight paths for your feet, so that what is lame may not be put out of joint but rather be healed.

The preacher has been using the illustration of a Grecian Olympian in his encouragement to persevere, even under divine chastisement. When training for combat, the instructor would deliver some serious blows to the trainee. He had to get him ready for the real deal. Only the truly committed would endure the challenge and be willing to be exercised in this way.[9] Of course, that is the point. If they couldn't make it through training, how were they going to have what it took for the anticipated day?

The preceding verse is obviously important here: "Now no chastening seems to be joyful for the present, but painful; nevertheless, afterward it yields the peaceable fruit of righteousness to those who have been trained by it" (NKJV). This fitness illustration gives me even more of an understanding of the Christian life. It involves struggle and wrestling, unceasing warfare, and many bruises. If we despair under the hard blows, we will not yield the peaceable fruit of righteousness. Like a good martial arts instructor, we need to encourage one another not to become weary under the blows.[10]

Also due to my family background, I'm a sucker for a good '80s karate flick. The main character is usually a student who has trained hard, repeating the same moves over and over, only with more chairs thrown in the room each time. Their instructor has revealed to them all their vulnerable weak spots with their own version of the faux-marker-sword. The trainee relies on the words and instruction of their "master" as they continue to raise their hands back up again and return to the fighting stance.

And then the big day approaches. In the end scene, their training is proving to be fruitful until some bad guy decides to cheat. And there they are, either with a broken leg from the Cobra Kai[11] or blinded by Chong Li,[12] left with a decision: Can they go on? Can they continue to fight? Usually this is when the fighter remembers all they have been training for. They have to rely on what they know to be true, what they have been

9. See Pink, *Exposition of Hebrews*, 984.

10. I will be discussing the teaching about discipline in this verse later in chapter 7.

11. See "Competition Begins," *The Karate Kid*, directed by John G. Avildsen (1984; Culver City, CA: Sony Pictures Home Entertainment, 2005), DVD.

12. See "Victory Out of Dust," *Bloodsport*, directed by Newt Arnold (1988; Burbank, CA: Warner Home Video, 2002), DVD.

exercising over and over. That's when they pull out the genius of the crane kick or fighting with a blindfold. Queue awesome '80s fighting music.

Theological fitness involves an exercising of the truths that we already have in Christ, constantly keeping our eye on the consummation of God's promises in his Son. Over and over again. And again. Don't let those arms fall! "Let us hold fast the confession of our hope without wavering, for he who promised is faithful." He is faithful to preserve us in the hard blows, as well as in the mundane repetitions of everyday life.

## EXTRA CHINS[13]

Speaking of the mundane, my days are packed with trivial drama. Solanna hid the toothpaste because Haydn (and probably Zaidee too) never puts the cap on when he's through. Between that and the over-squeezing, it gets all nasty (for extra effect Solanna says g-nasty). To solve this problem at first, I went from the one big tube to three 99-cent, trial-sized tubes. Problem not solved. Everyone claims the pristinely kept tube as his or her own. Solanna took matters into her own hands and hid the thing. What's a fourteen-year-old to do?

I tell myself to be happy they are all brushing their teeth.

My toothpaste example demonstrates that the trivial drama starts first thing in the morning, and keeps on going until it's time to brush their teeth again for bed. It's exhausting. When they were younger, I dreamt about the real conversations I would be having with my children by now throughout the day. Sure, there are plenty of those. My life is pretty wonderful, really. But sometimes it's the ordinary, inconsequential commotions that make me feel like a mama on the edge.

13. Someone with a "glass jaw" is easily knocked out in a fight by one blow to the jaw or chin. To have "extra chins" means the opposite. This is a fighter who can endure continuous blows to the face and still persevere. It seems like this fighter has extra chins in reserve, or an "iron chin."

There are books for this. However, I didn't give my children that much grace over the toothpaste incident. Sometimes the law just needs to be delivered with fear. Maybe it was a gospel-teaching moment that I forfeited, but my expired brain just wanted them to get over it, put the dang cap on, and go to bed! Really. That's it. I love the *idea* of having these gospel-teaching moments peppered throughout my day, but at some point my kids will turn even gospel talk into white noise if that's how I address every piece of craziness that they conjure up in a twenty-four-hour period.

And let's face it: I'm being selfish too—with my time, my sanity, and my desire not to be sucked into every bit of drama they want me to referee. Hooray for Solanna for independent problem solving. The other two knuckleheads will have to live with the consequences of *g*-nasty, clumpy toothpaste.

By this time my eye is twitching anyway and I'm the one who needs the gospel.

I want to talk to my kids about things that matter. I even want to goof off with them about a million things that don't matter. Most of all, I want them to know that the gospel matters all the time. It certainly puts things in perspective. "Jesus died for your filthy sins, every single one of them. He's given you his Holy Spirit as a seal to transform you into his image and guarantee you will be raised in new life. Who the heck cares about the toothpaste?" Or, "And you don't even want to share your clean toothpaste? What does that say about your heart?" Or, "And you can't even take care of a piddly tube of toothpaste? What does that say about your ungratefulness for all Christ has done for you?"

But I told you. I'm at the point of eye twitching and expiration. I'm perfectly happy to chalk it up to mom-fail. I have to pick my moments in the trivial war zone for when I'm going to deliver the gospel kablam-o,[14] because I still want it to have some kablam-o effect.

14. While Solanna invented *g-nasty*, I credit Zaidee for the word *kablam-o*.

And this is why I am happy to return to my corner between the tedious rounds of ordinary life in my day. I feel like the old guy who's trying to prove his tried and true skills in a comeback attempt. I may have a better reach, but those young'uns are relentless. I spend my days preparing for the big moves, uppercuts, submission holds, only to find that I'm barely cut out for the toothpaste round. I go to God's Word for extra chins. More often than not, it isn't the uppercut or the swing kick that does us in. It's the endless, inconsequential hits. As Joe Frazier said so well, "Kill the body and the head will die."[15]

Often, it's the small blows to the middle that wear us down. We just plain forget the good news. But the thing is, because of this announcement of Christ the Lord fulfilling all righteousness, we can hold fast with even more confidence to what is holy. Because he loved us even to the point of death, I can wholeheartedly affirm to my children that they are to love one another. And in these tedious rounds, I can return to God's promises for strength. When his Word ministers to us, we are strengthened to prevail because of our victorious Savior. He builds our endurance, which isn't built on manufactured conflict-resolution skills. As we exercise his graces in the small blows, we will be trained to put our hands up for the drop kicks in our future. And we can be confident that he who promised is faithful, and all this conditioning is making straight paths for our feet toward the Source of our strength in every blow.

## HOLDING FAST AT THE HIGHEST COST

Perhaps now you are thinking, "Great, I've invested almost three chapters of reading time into this book, and the most the author has ever had to overcome was trivial toothpaste encounters." Well, no, I have persevered through worse without

15. Joe Ryan attributes boxer Sam Langford as the origin of this quote Joe Frazier popularized in Joe Ryan, *Heavyweight Boxing in the 1970's: The Great Fighters and Rivalries* (Jefferson, NC: McFarland & Company: 2013), 67.

recanting my faith, but I haven't faced anything like Lady Jane Grey. This sixteen-year-old held fast to her confession with the worst of consequences. But my above illustration was important. The trivial issues that we deal with on a daily basis give us training and conditioning for turning again and again to the gospel.

If you are learning a musical instrument, you know that you have to go over the scales repeatedly. My son is constantly being tested on his basic math skills in the second grade. He gets all pumped up for the timed exams. In my brother's martial arts class, he has his expert fighters going over the basic jujitsu moves in repetitive drills. We know why this is so. To really master something, you have to go over the foundation at an obsessive level. Only then do you become free to play a beautiful song, solve one of those crazy "train left the station" word problems, or instinctively know how to avoid a rear naked choke in martial arts. So it is with the toothpaste moments. I am being shaped through the small obstacles, sanctified even as I am reminded of my own sin and my Savior's saving love for me. There's no other way but Christ, for the toothpaste rounds and for the threats of execution. Lady Jane knew this as a mere teenager.

I didn't realize when I was reading Simonetta Carr's biography on Lady Jane Grey to my kids that it was during the week marking the 458th anniversary of her execution. She was the Queen of England for nine days and was executed at sixteen years old, per order of the infamous "Bloody Mary." In this brief account of her life, a young reader will see some of the costs of true faith. It's easy to paint the Reformation in pastels to our children, but Carr doesn't do this. She shows the mess that went along with it. And in England, there were many political ramifications.

There's much about Lady Jane's story that glorifies the Lord. My reading of this condensed version with the kids coincided well with the study I had just taught on Hebrews 13:5–6. In these two verses, we are given some practical advice on holding fast.

> Let your conduct be without covetousness; be content with such things as you have. For He Himself has said, "I will never leave you or forsake you." So we may boldly say:
>
> > "The LORD is my helper;
> > I will not fear.
> > What can man do to me?" (NKJV)

Jane had plenty of circumstances that could have turned her into a covetous, complaining woman. As loved ones died, Jane held strong in the faith. She didn't seem to have the same inclinations as her parents, and their relationship was strained. And she had a very covetous cousin, Mary. It revealed itself in the worst kind of way when Mary's deathly ill stepbrother, King Edward, appointed Jane to be his successor to the throne. This wasn't really a position that Jane was ambitious for; however, she shared in Edward's passion for the Protestant faith to grow in England.

Jane was queen for only nine days before Mary and the supporters she had gathered took the crown that Mary believed was rightfully hers. As Jane's status went from queen to prisoner awaiting her fate, her faith only strengthened. As her family members were renouncing their Protestant faith and embracing Roman Catholicism to try to save their own lives, Jane refused. Jane was content with the lot God had given her. Her knowledge and faith astounded even the monk, John Feckenham, who was sent by Mary to convert Jane. The sixteen-year-old held her own theologically with the monk. Moments before her execution, Jane was able to share her witness to onlookers that she was dying "a true Christian woman" whose hope was "to be saved by none other means but only by the mercy of God and the merits of the blood of His only Son Jesus Christ."[16]

These words displayed the source of Jane's contentment. God preserved her to hold fast to the confession of her hope, even through the worst circumstances, because he really was her only helper. With the knowledge that God is faithful, and that he would never leave or forsake her, Jane echoed the last words of her Savior, "Lord, into thy hands I commend my spirit."[17]

The letters Jane wrote as she was preparing for her execution encouraged others that she was rejoicing in her impending death. She didn't just resign herself to her fate; rather, she found joy in God's will. Wherever she was called, Jane glorified the Lord who was with her. As she exercised the truths of who he is, Jane was strengthened to persevere. That's what I call theological fitness.

## BECAUSE HE IS HOLDING FAST

And yet, even Lady Jane's amazing fortitude to hold fast to the confession of her hope while facing extreme persecution is not sufficient to make us do so. Her testimony is encouraging to us because it points us to Jesus Christ, who sustains us. He is the one who truly held fast. His work in doing so is effectual for my own perseverance.

I was reflecting on this after a Maundy Thursday service I attended.[18] After a tasty, calorie-packed potluck meal, we remained in our seats at the fellowship hall tables to hear the pastor preach from Mark 15:16–47. He spent some time on verses 31 and 32, in which the chief priests and teachers of the law mocked Jesus. The pastor highlighted the fact that our Lord was ridiculed during his suffering on the cross. His

---

16. Simonetta Carr, *Lady Jane Grey* (Grand Rapids: Reformation Heritage Books, 2012), 52.

17. Ibid., 54.

18. Jerry Meade, "The King's Cross" (sermon, Pilgrim Presbyterian Church, Martinsburg, WV, March 28, 2013).

mockers said that the King of Kings should be able to get himself down, as if it were weakness that was keeping him up there. However, it was his strength that kept him holding fast. Jesus Christ stayed on that cross for us, because he trusted in the covenant that he had with his heavenly Father. Even as he cried out, "My God, my God, why have you forsaken me?," Jesus believed his Father's promise, and so he held on. And then, out of that trust, he was able to say, "Into your hands I commit my Spirit." We cannot even pretend to understand the theological, spiritual, emotional, and physical fitness this took.

The preacher to the Hebrews uses a nautical illustration to let us know that Christ our Lord is still holding fast for us. Encouraging the recipients of this sermon-letter to hold fast to God's promise, the preacher assures them that they can count on God's unchanging oath (Heb. 6:13–18). He then says,

> We have this as a sure and steadfast anchor of the soul, a hope that enters into the inner place behind the curtain, where Jesus has gone as a forerunner on our behalf, having become a high priest forever after the order of Melchizedek. (vv. 19–20)

What does an anchor do? It keeps the vessel from drifting away. And where are we told that Christ is anchored? Our Savior is a permanent anchor in the heavenly sanctuary.

This passage of Scripture combines all the flavors of theological fitness I have been focusing on, using the familiar spice from Psalm 110 that we will get to later. We have the exhortation to hold fast the confession of our hope (v. 18), the fitness metaphor of the race (v. 20), and the Psalm 110 trifecta (v. 20). Kablam-o! This reference to Jesus as our High Priest reminds the reader of Christ's rested position at the right hand of the Father. He isn't getting up until all of his enemies are as a footstool to him. It is encouraging and assuring for us to have this anchor metaphor of our Savior.

An anchor is doing its job when it isn't seen. Instead of being in the earthly temple, full of the types and shadows that the Hebrews could see and touch, Christ is anchored in the heavenly sanctuary, the real archetype that the earthly temple merely copied. He's holding fast to us, preserving our faith through every kind of weather by means of his continuous intercession with the Father.

Dennis Johnson sums up our ultimate hope well for us as it's presented in Hebrews.

> Those who long for lasting security need a hope anchored in heaven itself (6:19), an ever-living priest who never needs replacement (7:24) serving in an eternal sanctuary not constructed by human hands (8:2; 9:11), a once-for-all sacrifice that needs no repetition (10:11–14), and a future city founded by God himself and therefore sure to last, unlike Jerusalem and its Temple, which would soon lie in ruins (11:10; 13:14).[19]

When it is presented to us this way, of course we are motivated to hold fast in obedience to the faith. It is our privilege. Our great Captain himself anchors us. He will lose none.

## GOING THE EXTRA MILE

1. Why is it such a struggle to hold fast to your hope? When is it particularly more difficult for you to hold fast to your confession?

2. Do you find that you tend to be easily distracted or persuaded to give up on the whole Christian life?

3. Are you more tempted to look to your own successes and accomplishments in order to persevere than to God's promises in Christ? Do your failures send you into despair that you may not finish the race?

19. Dennis E. Johnson, *Him We Proclaim: Preaching Christ from All the Scriptures* (Phillipsburg, NJ: P&R, 2007), 195.

4. Do you have a plan for theological training? How could you get a plan together or help someone else in discipleship? What unanswered questions do you have about Christianity that you may want to investigate? Is there a doctrine that you have wanted to learn more about?

5. Often I have well-meaning friends who confess that they just aren't good readers. They also may have trouble focusing on the sermon. What are some methods that can help teach someone to be more engaged before, during, and after they read or sit under the preached Word?

6. Hebrews 12:12 acknowledges the heavy blows that we all encounter. But it doesn't excuse our staying down. How can we be encouragers of the gospel to one another at these times?

7. See this chapter's definition of having "extra chins"—what does it mean to have extra chins in the Christian life? How is this analogy important for both the heavy blows and the trivial, mundane matters that may wear us down? What kind of conditioning does a Christian train under for extra chins (think '80s karate movies)?

8. How does it put things in perspective when we think of the image that Hebrews 6 gives us of Christ being our anchor in the heavenly sanctuary? Who's the One really holding on?

# | 4 |

# THEOLOGICAL CONDITIONING

Being superabundantly engaged in our confession of hope is quite a task. In fact, for the past three chapters I have been alluding that it takes theological fitness. In this chapter I would like to highlight this particular fitness that all Christians have, and are exhorted to exercise as they hold fast in perseverance. Here we will finally get to the details of that marathon I keep referring to as well.

In a study on the doctrine of Christ, my Sunday school teacher asked a question that stuck with me. Our text was Hebrews 12:1–2,

> Therefore, since we are surrounded by so great a cloud of witnesses, let us also lay aside every weight, and sin which clings so closely, and let us run with endurance the race that is set before us, looking to Jesus, the founder and perfecter of our faith, who for the joy that was set before him endured the cross, despising the shame, and is seated at the right hand of the throne of God.

The question: How is the death of Christ an example of patient endurance?

Of course, there are several obvious answers, and I could quickly write down what the text provided: "for the joy that was set before him." What a profound statement! I've been chewing on the relationship of patient endurance and joy ever since. This connection is what ultimately led to a whole book about theological fitness.

We don't really like the words *patient* or *endure*. My Strong's Concordance breaks down the Greek *endured* with words like "to stay under, remain, bear, have fortitude, persevere, abide, and patiently suffer."[1] In my mind, many of these synonyms sound like a passive survival. But no one I know would say, "I hope to passively survive my Christian life."

The preacher to the Hebrews compares our Christian life to running a race. He points us to a cloud of witnesses who have forged ahead by faith, receiving their future hope. More importantly, he points us to Jesus Christ, whose patient endurance was active for the sake of joy. I've been thinking a lot about the fitness of Jesus lately. He did not give up his life until the proper time. Think of how he must have longed to be with his Father in heaven. But, even stronger, he patiently endured for joyful submission to his Father in fulfilling an oath to redeem a people for himself. Jesus had to give up his life; it could not be taken from him.

Quite clearly, none of us could even begin to run if it were not for the author and finisher of our faith. Not one of us has the fitness required to bear the curse of the world's sin on that tree. Only the Son of God would be qualified as a contender. In his earthly ministry, he fulfilled all righteousness, resisted temptation, and was ready to be both our sin offering and our thank offering. Even as the God-man, Jesus found that drinking the cup of God's wrath was enough to make him fall to the ground (see Matt. 26:39). Jeremiah Burroughs lamented about the weight our Savior bore as he fell on his face in prayer.

He, who upholds the heavens and the earth by His power, now falls groveling upon the earth, having the weight and

---

1. James Strong, LLD., STD, *The New Strong's Exhaustive Concordance of the Bible* (Nashville: Thomas Nelson Publishers, 1990), Strong's number 5278.

burden of man's sin upon Him. . . . If all the strength of all the men who ever lived since the beginning of the world, and all the angels in heaven, were put into one, and he had only that weight upon him that Christ had, it would have made him sink down into eternal despair; for had not Christ been God as well as man, He could never have borne it, but would have sunk down eternally.[2]

Only one man had the ability to endure—Jesus Christ.

Because of this, we are told to run with endurance the race set before us. Only Jesus had the fitness for the cross, but because of him believers are given the fitness for the Christian life. Only Jesus was qualified for the work of our salvation. But he has now qualified us for holiness. Fitness requires conditioning, and we are exhorted to actively endure. Most of us are familiar with exercise, whether we enjoy it or not. The preacher to the Hebrews uses exercise as a great metaphor for perseverance. I think of the cloud of witnesses as the "before" and "after" shots that fitness programs use for promotions. We are given a real testimony of believers who endured. My "before" shot is pretty shabby. But my "after" shot will be a glorified, resurrected body!

As simple as it may be to begin a race, you need to have the stamina to finish. Anyone can make a profession, but not all who profess the Lord will join him in the great eschatological feast. By God's grace, Christians are given endurance to persevere to the end as his Spirit conditions us and strengthens our faith along the way.

Most people feel pretty strong in the beginning of a workout. But once our body temperature rises, our hearts beat faster, and our breathing becomes more laborious, we begin to feel pretty weak. In one workout DVD I own, the fitness trainer likes to lay on the heavy licking in the end. He reminds us that the

2. Jeremiah Burroughs, *The Evil of Evils*, ed. Don Kistler (repr., Morgan, PA: Soli Deo Gloria Publications, 1990), 100.

physically fit need to finish strong. As we begin our weighted-side-plank-T-stand-pushup craziness, the fitness models begin crying out for mercy (that's when you know it's bad). The trainer smiles and encourages, "I am with you." I always think of how Jesus told his disciples the same thing in his Great Commission (Matt. 28:18–20). Every Christian can finish strong because the finisher of our faith finished strong. He really is with us through his Spirit, the preaching of his Word, and the administration of his sacraments. I can do all things through Jesus Christ, who strengthens me (see Phil. 4:13) and is the joy who is set before me.

## THE AGONY OF FITNESS

The thing is, even the fit have to suffer. In fact, the fitness-inclined intentionally suffer for the greater glory. Let's take our marathon analogy from Hebrews. No matter how much you may train, running a marathon is no easy task. Actually, the more conditioned you are, the better idea you have of the suffering that you are about to embark on. This is why we aren't all signing up for the next long-distance race that passes through town. The truly fit do not have a false confidence in their abilities. They know what it takes to make it to the end.

We really cannot comprehend what Christ endured on the cross. We have no idea what it takes to bear the full wrath of God for our sin. We can't even handle the full disclosure of the deceit of our own hearts. God is patient in maturing us through his Word and Spirit even as he progressively unveils our sin to us in sanctification. But Jesus, although sinless, knew the cost. We see this as he prayed in the garden of Gethsemane,

> saying, "Father, if you are willing, remove this cup from me. Nevertheless, not my will, but yours, be done." And there appeared to him an angel from heaven, strengthening him. And being in an agony he prayed more earnestly; and his sweat became like great drops of blood falling down to the ground. (Luke 22:42–44)

We know that as the Christ, Jesus had the fitness to endure the cross. But we see a vulnerable picture of his sinless humanity here in Luke. There's something interesting about this prayer. As Christ sees the affliction before him, he submits to the Father's will in obedience *before* he is strengthened to continue. He prays in anguish for another way, obeys his call, and *then* an angel is sent to strengthen him. That is the epitome of theological fitness. We see a fighting faith in Christ's prayer. Jesus is actively engaging in prayer and exercising his faith, and he perseveres because of his intimate knowledge of the Father. He trusts in the promise. That is his joy—a joy worth the cost. Something my previous pastor pointed out in a sermon on Mark 14, titled "Seeing Clearly," applies here so fittingly as well: "Christ can see the hand of God at work, knowing that not one blow will fall on him unnecessarily for our salvation."[3] That is holding fast the confession of your hope without wavering, knowing that he who promised really is faithful.

> In the days of his flesh, Jesus offered up prayers and supplications, with loud cries and tears, to him who was able to save him from death, and he was heard because of his reverence. Although he was a son, he learned obedience through what he suffered. (Heb. 5:7–8)

David Allen notes how similar this verse from Hebrews is to the description of the account that is given in Luke. Both emphasize the suffering and humanity of Christ and his ability to truly relate to us as our high priest. "It is only in Heb 5:8 and Luke 2:52 that we have a statement regarding Jesus' inner human development."[4] These verses also connect our

---

3. Jerry Meade, "Seeing Clearly" (sermon, Pilgrim Presbyterian Church, Martinsburg, WV, March 10, 2013).

4. David L. Allen, *Lukan Authorship of Hebrews* (Nashville: B&H, 2010), 203.

marathon analogy in chapter 12 with the agony of fitness and theological stamina.

> W.R. Paton suggested that the Greek word *agōnia* was often used to describe the kind of agony that a runner experienced in an athletic contest prior to the start of a race, and that this meaning best fits Luke 22:44 . . .
>
> The parallel to Heb 5:7–10; 6:20 (where Jesus is said to be the "forerunner") and also to 12:1–2 (where the same Greek word *agōnia* occurs) is unmistakable. In Heb 12:1, the race is said to be *ton prokeimenon hēmin agōna*, "the race that lies before us." This same participle is used again in v. 2 in reference to the "joy" that "lay before Him." The implication is that God set the joy before Jesus and thus set the race before us.[5]

Think about it. Christ, who had the fitness to obey the Father's will, prayed in agony. He knew the cost. He felt the cost. As he depended on the Father through the Sprit, we see that he was strengthened to complete his mission. Particularly, he was motivated by joy to patiently endure. We are told to look to Jesus, who is our joy, to run the race set before us. He's gone ahead. The same Spirit that sent angels to strengthen Jesus to finish has applied his victorious work to his people. We can finish! Sure, he knows we will fall. But he's got it covered. He is with us. He will take us to the end.

Another thing is clear. It will be through the path of suffering. We may not be signing up for the local race in town, but every Christian has a marathon to run. And running a marathon is no passive endeavor. We will be strengthened; we will be changed.

## MENTAL FITNESS

Clearly there is much conditioning ahead in our sanctification process. To be sure, God is preserving us through the race.

5. Ibid., 204.

But anyone who's ever been involved in any exercise program, or ever had to do a fitness test for a phys. ed. class, knows why the author of Hebrews uses this metaphor.

Continual exercise leads to physical fitness. This is an aspiration of mine because I want to be ready, able, and free to *do* whatever opportunity may come before me. My husband and I are approaching that awkward stage in parenting when we notice that our children are becoming increasingly physically apt while our own fitness levels have been on the decline. If my daughters challenge me to a backyard showdown, my goal is to be ready to clean their clocks (or at least keep up with them!). As our son grows, Matt wants to continue to be the man to beat at a game of hoops. We want to enjoy bike rides, hiking, and other outdoor activities with our kids. We don't want our fitness levels to prohibit us from relishing life's moments, or even from protecting our family if need be. To keep up with the increasing physical abilities of our children, we need to condition ourselves in continual exercise.

Likewise, our spiritual life requires much fitness. Peter tells us to "always [be] prepared to make a defense to anyone who asks you for a reason for the hope that is in you" (1 Peter 3:15). He gives this exhortation in the context of suffering for God's truth. There are two qualifications of fitness here: knowing God's truth, and the patient endurance of suffering for the sake of it. This requires conditioning, strengthening, and training.

Just as our bodies need continual practice in any kind of physical training, so do our minds in theological growth. We are talking about a mental fitness here. Do you like to learn? Theology refers to a knowledge of God. You may not be a professional theologian, but you do have some sort of knowledge of God, whether it is true or false. How do we expect to run the race with endurance if we do not know the One we are running to? A race has a path with boundaries leading to a particular destination. If we do not know our destination, how are we assured it is the right one? How will we be prepared to suffer for his name if we do not treasure it above all the world offers? What if, in the end, we hear, "I never knew you; depart from me" (see Matt. 7:23; 25:41; Heb. 6:7–8)?

This is why Romans 12:2 is one of my favorite verses of Scripture: "Do not be conformed to this world, but be trans-formed by the renewal of your mind, that by testing you may discern what is the will of God, what is good and acceptable and perfect." We are always learning, whether it is purposeful or passive. What are you filling your mind with—meat or fat?

The preacher to the Hebrews cracks a pretty strong whip on this question. He is ready to move on and teach them about the priestly order of Melchizedek, but they are still hung up on the basics of the faith. He is pretty much telling them that they have become too lazy to listen and accuses them of being "dull of hearing."

> For though by this time you ought to be teachers, you need someone to teach you again the basic principles of the oracles of God. You need milk, not solid food, for everyone who lives on milk is unskilled in the word of righteousness, since he is a child. But solid food is for the mature, for those who have their powers of discernment trained by constant practice to distinguish good from evil. (5:12–14)

The Bible reveals to us everything we need to know about God and equips us for training in righteousness (2 Tim. 3:16–17). Our knowledge of God shapes our desire and our will. Jesus' prayer in Gethsemane reveals the wrestling match that this can be. But we need to ask ourselves if we even have the proper knowledge of God to draw from when our faith is challenged. This laziness isn't just hurting ourselves. The writer chides the Hebrews for being unprofitable to others. We might not all teach a Sunday school class or a Bible study, but as we mature, we all have a responsibil-ity to bring benefit to others with our knowledge of God.

Our verses of reprimand above are written in the context of warning against apostasy. Our faith will be challenged. Every day we are tempted to disobedience. But here we see the preacher to the Hebrews highlighting the importance of the fitness of our minds to defend us from falling away from the faith. We need to *know* what we know and how to use it.

## IT'S IN THE BAG

Way before mixed martial arts became all the rage, my father taught self-defense tactics. He has black belts in several different forms of martial arts and he was a Secret Service agent for a while. Dad combined his knowledge from these different methods to teach self-defense. The martial arts is not just a physical sport; it is a way of thinking. As a student, you become disciplined to anticipate, be aware of your surroundings, discern different paths of escape when threatened, and have a readiness to fight for the defense of yourself or others as a last resort. There is an honor that is taught in defending another person. This kind of thinking was ingrained in me since childhood.

One summer while I was home from college, I was taking my dad's women's self-defense class. Dad had a creative method to his teaching. I particularly remember one lesson when he had us go get our purses and bring them to the mat. One dangerous scenario that women need to have a heightened awareness for is when they are walking to their car alone. This is when we are a bit more vulnerable as a target. Oftentimes we will be carrying a purse. That lesson was spent learning how to use items that were already in our purse as self-defense weapons.

Keys are a great tool for defense. We have those wonderful alarms that can deter an attack at the push of a button. So it is a great idea for a woman to go ahead and walk with her keys in hand before she leaves the store, restaurant, or home she is visiting. Instead of being vulnerable as you rummage with your head down for your keys, be ready. Dad taught us how to hold our keys with one laced between each finger. If I did need to throw a punch, this one would maybe do enough damage to buy me some running time—because the goal is to flee, not to duke it out with a man who can overpower you. We also learned how to use pens to gouge eyes, and the whole purse itself as a propeller to hit a man where it hurts. I have a visual memory of my dad taking one woman's magazine, rolling it up, and smacking the heck out of the punching bag with it. Good times.

Now I am seeing blaring theological connections. What *do* we have? There is a certain type of intelligence in even being able to take an inventory. Just last night, my husband and I were watching television together. I used the bathroom during a commercial break, and when I returned, Matt said to me, "I thought you went to the other bathroom. When I saw a dark silhouette coming from that side of the house, it startled me, and I thought about how vulnerable I am sitting in this chair." Immediately my instincts kicked in and I commented, "Well, you could start by throwing the glass in your hand to startle him, and that will give you the chance to get up . . ." I'm not so sure my husband welcomed fighting advice from his wife, but my mind has been ingrained to catalog my resources and anticipate how they may be utilized.

This illustration raises the question, "What's in your theological bag?" Although Dad was showing us how to use everyday items for defense, I wasn't going to get very far with a Kleenex or a pack of gum. The preacher to the Hebrews was upset at the theological content in the minds of his readers. Because they were not learning more from God's Word and becoming equipped for the Christian life of obedience to God and service to others, he accused them of not having very much to draw from. Just milk, no meat. How was this group going to endure the persecution ahead with such poor theological readiness?

The preacher anticipated the likelihood of apostasy for those who profess Christ's name now but have not bothered to really know him. Who is willing to suffer for a Savior they won't even trouble themselves to learn about?

As I condition myself in learning, I pray for wisdom. For proper training and conditioning, I need to put myself under the preaching of God's Word, alongside others who are in the race. As we receive Christ and all his benefits together, we are strengthened, ready to live accordingly and share our faith with others. We are equipped by the truth, thereby able to identify the false. Our Father transforms us by his grace, through his Word and the power of his Spirit. As my knowledge of God increases, so does my joy in serving him. As the fitness level of my mind rises, he combines my knowledge and experiences to produce wisdom. Even when the apparent injuries come, the joy remains through suffering. Why? Because I know that my salvation is based on what Christ has already done, not in my own abilities. In him I find my meaning and my value. For this reason, I have confident hope as I strive to hear, at the finish line, "Well done, my good and faithful servant" (see Matt. 25:21).

## ARE YOU EVEN IN THE RACE, OR ARE YOU MISSING OUT?

Not only do we need to be growing in knowledge, we need to be growing in the right knowledge. It will do us no good to be running hard and steady to the wrong finish line. These days there are so many competitors vying for our attention. It is easy to get distracted and veer off course.

Apparently, I'm terribly bad at the hustle. I have a modest blog that I try to update about two or three times a week. Sometimes I think about incorporating a better strategy to gain a wider audience of readers. There's a plethora of blogs out there full of advice about blogging and writing. It seems that so many of these websites are filled with people selling eBooks that hold the six secrets you need to write a bestseller. Or, if I just spend $3.99, I can instantly download the three things that are keeping my blog from reaching the tens of thousands of people who need to be reading it. I haven't been very good about scattering my seed all over Twitter or even setting up a *Housewife Theologian* Facebook page to then ask people to "like." But that's only the beginning. One of the key ways to draw people to your site, I'm told, is to make the title, or the Tweet's "sell," give readers a sense that they are missing out on something. That's it—appeal to the collective fear of the unassuming social media perusers that they are not down with the latest. There's actually a term for this proclivity to be in the know. It's called FOMO—Fear Of Missing Out.

We're all chasing the new—that one more thing that we might be missing. Some will camp out overnight in line to be the first with the latest. We check our status updates and news tickers to be the first to hear who said what, and why what so-and-so says about it is so important.

This is what I was thinking about as our Sunday school class was reading and discussing Acts 17:16–32, in which Paul addresses the Areopagus. The men of Athens were eager to hear this new doctrine that Paul was babbling about in the synagogue and marketplace. Paul astutely notices the attention he is receiving for teaching something "new," and even appeals to it. He notices the fear that the Athenians had of neglecting to appease a god they might not know. Paul, in what seems to be an almost mocking tone, affirms to them that they are a very religious people. And, look at that, they even have an altar TO THE UNKNOWN GOD. The council at Mars Hill wanted to make sure they had all their bases covered. They did not want to be missing out on the latest. There was always going to be the "one more thing" that might be worthy of worship.

It seems ironic to us that the supposed knowledge capital of the ancient world would be so wrapped up in appeasing gods of every area of life, especially with these superfluous altars. My own logic laughs at a god with a lowercase "g." If you were a god, then you would need to be God, sovereign over everything, not just a god over fertility, leisure, money, or science. These supposed deities of the Greek pantheon sound pretty weak and unworthy of worship.

Well, that is exactly what Paul points out as he endeavors to tell the men of the council not about "one more thing," as their extra altar might suggest, but about "the only thing," the one true God. Of course, there is so much to glean from these verses about how Paul uses general revelation and quotes from their own poets to evangelize these sophisticated pagans. And yet most of those pagans are disappointed to hear that Paul is introducing not a new god, but the God of old who makes all things new.

Things get uncomfortable when Paul moves to the crux of his argument. As he cleverly lays the foundation of the one true God, he then moves to the resurrection question that they had asked him about. This is a repugnant doctrine to the Greeks. Most of them have heard enough, and he is cut off. But a few do believe.

So often, even as believers, we fall into this insatiable desire to hear the new. We must appease the latest news god. Clever marketing has caught on to our proclivities and exploited them. They tell us what we are to desire. Paul also honed in on this tendency, but he didn't sell what the Athenians really wanted to hear. Most of them wanted to stick with the lowercase gods.

Since our God of old is the uppercase God, there are always new attributes that we will discover about him. We don't need a bazillion little "g's" to satisfy our longing to learn and worship. Since he is God, we will spend eternity getting to know him without ever exhausting our knowledge. It's both exciting and humbling to learn more about our God. He isn't manageable. He isn't appeased by our own creative ideas of how to worship him. There is only one way to approach God, and that is by grace through faith. In case you missed out, the Messiah has come. Jesus Christ has fulfilled all righteousness, propitiated God's wrath for our sin, and risen from the dead. It is finished.

Therefore the only path to the finish line of glory is the path of grace. We are told that those who find it are few (Matt. 7:14). Every path has a god at the end of it. We run toward what we worship. Many opt to run a course of their own righteousness. But God has already shown us that we are incapable of this. When God delivered the law on Mt. Sinai, his voice shook the earth. We are told that the Israelites couldn't endure the commandments. "Indeed, so terrifying was the sight that Moses said, 'I tremble with fear'" (Heb. 12:21). The law reveals the holiness of God and our complete impotence. Thankfully, it also points to a Savior who fulfilled its every demand.

There are really only two, mountainous paths. One is to try to earn our own holiness through the law, the track of Mt. Sinai. The other is to run clothed in the righteousness of another, to the glorious Mt. Zion. We do not earn a spot; we receive it by the gospel.

> Therefore let us be grateful for receiving a kingdom that cannot be shaken, and thus let us offer to God acceptable worship, with reverence and awe, for our God is a consuming fire. (Heb. 12:28–29)

In this path to Mt. Zion, the law then becomes our friend, guiding us to the finish line of holiness. We can now offer acceptable worship to the one true God in Spirit and in truth.

## THEOLOGY AND A TICKET TO RIDE

Hopefully I have been building a good case that what we know about God, our theology, affects our Christian walk. This is certainly true regarding perseverance. Christians have many ideas about how we prevail to the end. Maybe you are asking these questions as you read along: "How can we know that we will make it to the finish line? Do I have the fitness required to persevere?"

One idea I absorbed growing up goes along with the "once saved, always saved" doctrine. I think this doctrine has good intentions toward assurance of salvation, but expects way too little from the faithfulness of God. The implications can lead to what seems like a double life. Assured that praying "the prayer of salvation" gives you your permanent ticket to heaven, this theology appears to have God locked in. The necessity of becoming an actual disciple who is being transformed into the image of Christ becomes a mere suggestion. Many opt to maybe get to that part later, and really don't wrestle with sin. For them, perseverance isn't like a race at all, but like a confidence in their own words, and maybe in the way they felt when they prayed them.

But God is faithful to finish what he began (Phil. 1:6). If he has drawn a sinner to himself in repentance to salvation, this faith will produce fruit. This fruit includes a love for righteousness and a hatred of sin. I'm not going to be dragged through the race unchanged, but the process usually looks a lot like a wrestling match in the believer's life. So while I believed that Christians couldn't lose their salvation, I was noticing some holes in this "once saved, always saved" doctrine.

As I began mingling with other Christians in my early twenties, I saw a different idea regarding perseverance. Some of my new friends did not believe in assurance of salvation. They believed that their sin could forfeit their salvation. This teaching also has a low view of the faithfulness of God. Its focus is on the faithfulness of the believer. I noticed that these friends of mine had a very deceiving idea about their own righteousness. While they often talked about how wonderful the Lord is, they had some very strict, legalistic boundaries to "keep them in the faith." I wondered, What kind of God was this? Does our God give his promises with conditions attached? I knew I wasn't righteous enough to keep my salvation going on my own. If this view of perseverance were true, I would be living my life in the wrong kind of fear.

And yet I think both of these views have a piece of truth in them. God's promises are real; he never goes back on them. We can be assured of this. And, once you have faith, you will not be the same. You will love righteousness and persevere.

But both of these views of perseverance are man-focused. The first one focuses on the words that you pray, and maybe in the sincerity or feeling you had when you prayed them. The second focuses on your faithfulness, your avoidance of sin, and your own works of righteousness.

In his *Institutes of the Christian Religion*, John Calvin explains beautifully, "He who truly believes can never fall away."[6] Calvin goes to God's Word and explains how

> Paul [cf. 1 Cor. 10:12] does not discourage Christians from simple confidence but rather from crass and sheer confidence in the flesh, which bears in its train haughtiness, arrogance, and contempt of others, snuffs out humility and reverence for God, and makes one forget grace received. . . . He also requires fear, not that we may be dismayed and waver but that, as we have stated elsewhere, in preparing us humbly to receive God's grace, our trust in him may be no wise diminished.[7]

Perseverance is humbling. We desire righteousness, but we fall on our faces. We look forward to the promise of eternally dwelling with God in holiness, and yet we know how far we are from it. We receive God's grace knowing that we are so utterly undeserving. We don't persevere by looking to ourselves. And

6. John Calvin, *Institutes of the Christian Religion*, ed. John McNeill (Louisville: Westminster John Knox Press, n.d.), 973.

7. Ibid.

this is where Calvin's teaching on the matter is so comforting. "Christ, then, is the mirror wherein we must, and without self-deception may, contemplate our own election."[8] Sure, we will doubt that we have what it takes to persevere to the end. That's because we don't.

But Christ has already done the work for us, as the author and finisher of our faith. All our promises are in Christ; praise God! He had the fitness to persevere, and he is now preserving his own through his Holy Spirit to run to the end. We will fall as we battle the flesh. But we get back up again. Because of the grace we have been given in Christ, we look to him and love righteousness. We see his work on the cross and we hate sin. We can confidently run into our Father's arms in repentance.

In Christ, we do have a ticket to ride. We have the ticket to run the race in the first place. When we look to our Savior, we see him sitting at the right hand of the throne of God. We can be assured that we will persevere, because we see our preservation as a gift. And all that the Father has given him, he will never cast out (John 6:37).

## GOING THE EXTRA MILE

1. How can perseverance be a gift and yet not be a passive endeavor?

2. How are both joy and agony set before us in the marathon that is the Christian life?

3. How does what we know to be true about God help us in our most vulnerable moments? What particular Scriptures would be helpful for you to memorize for your struggles in perseverance?

4. Do you sometimes find it more difficult to pray when you are weighed down with a heavy burden? What does Jesus' prayer in Luke 22:42–44 reveal about the way we can

8. Ibid., 970.

approach God in these difficult times? What can we expect as a result?

5. Read John 10:17–18. What does this statement tell us about both the authority and the obedience of Christ? How do you think this knowledge helped him as he prayed in Gethsemane? How does it help us now as we pray for perseverance?

6. How would you evaluate the theological state of the evangelical church today? Do a little research on the top ten bestselling Christian books listed by Amazon or some other popular bookseller. What is the quality of teaching about God? How can you have better discernment in finding good teaching? What have you been filling your mind with? Why is this important?

7. Read 1 Peter 3:13–17. How do these verses speak to our theological stamina? What two things should you expect after reading them?

8. Where might you see FOMO revealing itself in your own life? What other idols might you be chasing down when you give into this proclivity? How is theological conditioning important here?

9. If Christ is the mirror of our election, what does this say about our perseverance? What happens when we look to something else to help us endure?

## PART 3

# "THE CONFESSION OF OUR HOPE"

# JESUS IS LORD IN HIS PERSON

Have you ever started a workout when you were out of shape? Or maybe you are a conditioned runner and decided to give weights a try for the first time. Perhaps you love cruising on your bike, but you changed things up with some basketball. If you just aren't inclined to physical fitness of any kind, what would it be like if you decided to go on a hike with your friends? Two things happen. First, your body is shocked during the workout. You're not used to breathing that heavily or exerting that specific level of energy. The workout is harder than you expected. And the second effect usually comes around the second and third day—you are sore! The sermon-letter to the Hebrews may be like that.

My task in the next two chapters is to lay down the crux of our verse, the confession of our hope. It's interesting that the preacher to the Hebrews reprimands his readers for their theological immaturity, lamenting that he is having to give them milk instead of meat (5:11–14), yet many today find this sermon to be more theological meat than they can handle. Like a first workout, this chapter may be a gauge of your spiritual fitness level. You may see which muscles have been exercised well and which you may have been neglecting. So get your sneakers on.

## CHRISTIANS, WHAT DO YOU BELIEVE?

Christians, what *do* you believe? Every communion Sunday, my pastor asks the congregation this question. In unison, we confess the Apostles' Creed. Christians have been faithfully reciting this creed for over fifteen hundred years. Do you know what you believe? Remember that motto from the White Horse Inn that I mentioned in the introduction: "Know what you believe, and why you believe it"?[1] Theology aims to answer both the *what* and the *why* by studying the *Who*. If we are to hold fast to the confession of our hope to persevere in the Christian life, we'd better know what that confession is. Do you struggle to articulate the content of your faith? What is it that you cling to when your faith is challenged—a feeling that you have? An experience? Your own good works? The way that you were raised? The people that you associate with?

Christianity is a historic faith that has content. There are certain elements to our confession that would devastate our faith if they were not true. The apostle Paul himself labors this point in 1 Corinthians 15 and concludes, "If the dead are not raised, 'Let us eat and drink, for tomorrow we die'" (v. 33). Hope is not the same as wishful thinking; it is based on truth. Hebrews is chock full of the essentials of the Christian faith. In it, we will find that all of the Old Testament types were pedagogically pointing to the true Archetype, Jesus Christ. He is the true Prophet, the true Priest, and the true King. Hallelujah!

We are all theologians and we all have a creed. The question is, are we good theologians or bad ones? Theology is simply the study of who God is, and that is something everyone wrestles with, even the atheist (as proven by the term *atheism*). As soon as you begin to answer the question of who he is, you are giving a creed. Some Christians like to say that they hold to no creed but the Bible, but this isn't exactly an honest answer. As Carl Trueman points out,

> Christians are not divided between those who have creeds and confessions and those who do not; rather, they are divided

1. See "About Us," White Horse Inn, accessed March 6, 2015, http://www.whitehorseinn.org.

between those who have public creeds and confessions that are written down and exist as public documents, subject to public scrutiny, evaluation, and critique, and those who have private creeds and confessions that are often improvised, unwritten, and thus not open to public scrutiny, not susceptible to evaluation and, crucially and ironically, not, therefore, subject to testing by Scripture to see whether they are true.[2]

Throughout history, the church has labored to preserve an orthodox profession of what a Christian believes. Creeds serve like maps to the Word of God, helping us to comprehensively understand its teachings.

The confession of our hope is the gospel. The short version is, "Jesus is Lord!" But to quote Trueman again, "Arguably, all of Christian theology is simply one long running commentary upon, or fleshing out of, this short, simple, ecstatic cry."[3] Amen. Let's get to it.

Who is Jesus? Jesus is Lord! Hebrews 1:3 tells us, "He is the radiance of the glory of God and the exact imprint of his nature, and he upholds the universe by the word of his power." In this verse we have two profound statements about Jesus. Richard Phillips elucidates, "We see Jesus as Lord both in his person and in his work."[4] This is something worth reflecting on. So I thought I would use the help of David, a Puritan, and the sermon-letter to the Hebrews to elaborate on our confession. In this chapter we are going to focus on who Jesus is. In the following chapter we will look at what he has done, what he is doing, and what he will do. He is Lord in it all.

## DAVID'S CREED

Since this book is about theological fitness, I thought I'd give myself a little challenge in presenting our confession of

2. Carl R. Trueman, *The Creedal Imperative* (Wheaton, IL: Crossway, 2012), 15.

3. Trueman, *Creedal Imperative*, 136.

4. Richard D. Phillips, *Hebrews* (Phillipsburg, NJ: P&R, 2006), 18.

hope. The preacher would not exhort the Hebrews to hold fast to a confession that he hadn't already faithfully delivered. What sort of creed do we find in the sermon-letter to the Hebrews?

Recent scholarship has suggested that Hebrews may in fact be a sermon based on Psalm 110—a "homiletic midrash [interpretation]"[5] of sorts. Puritan Edward Reynolds (1599–1676) referred to Psalm 110 as "'symbolum Davidicum', the prophet David's creed."[6] So I thought, "Why not use Reynolds's format of the Christian confessions from Psalm 110 to organize the confession of our hope elaborated for us so greatly in the sermon-letter to the Hebrews?"

Psalm 110 is the psalm most quoted in the New Testament. And yet it is quite brief, composed of only seven verses. However, you can't carry these seven verses in your back pocket. No way; these words are far weightier than they might look at first glance. Reynolds suggests fourteen crucial confessions of the faith from this one psalm, which he claims to be "one of the clearest and most compendious prophesies of the person and offices of Christ in the whole Old Testament."[7] The New Testament writers must have thought the same, since they quoted it so often in teaching the faith. Those confessions are: the doctrine of the Trinity, the incarnation, the sufferings of Christ, his completed work, resurrection, ascension and intercession, a holy catholic Church, communion of saints, the last judgment and day of his wrath, remission of sins, resurrection of the body, and life everlasting.[8]

The confessions that Reynolds pulls out of Psalm 110 are not in the order of the verses. Consequently, I think it would

---

5. George Wesley Buchanan, *To the Hebrews* (AB 36; Garden City: Doubleday, 1972), xix, quoted in Dennis E. Johnson, *Him We Proclaim: Preaching Christ from All the Scriptures* (Phillipsburg, NJ: P&R, 2007), 178.

6. Edward Reynolds, *The Whole Works of Right Rev. Edward Reynolds*, Google Books, vol. 2 (London: 1826), 7. Available online at http://books.google.com/books?id=ooEAAAAAMAAJ&dq=related%3AOXFORD600004748&pg=PR1#v=onepage&q&f=false.

7. Ibid.

8. Ibid, 7–8.

be prudent for me to begin by quoting the psalm in full so that it will be easier for you, the reader, to refer back to as we go along. As I then expound upon each confession of "David's creed," I will mainly be using the sermon-letter to the Hebrews to guide us.

> The LORD says to my Lord:
>     "Sit at my right hand,
> until I make your enemies your footstool."

> The LORD sends forth from Zion
>     your mighty scepter.
>     Rule in the midst of your enemies!
> Your people will offer themselves freely
>     on the day of your power,
>     in holy garments;
> from the womb of the morning,
>     the dew of your youth will be yours.
> The LORD has sworn
>     and will not change his mind,
> "You are a priest forever
>     in the order of Melchizedek."

> The Lord is at your right hand;
>     he will shatter kings on the day of his wrath.
> He will execute judgment among the nations,
>     filling them with corpses;
> he will shatter chiefs
>     over the wide earth.
> He will drink from the brook by the way;
>     therefore he will lift up his head.

Some of this language may sound difficult to understand. Like me, you may have read right past this psalm countless times without reflecting upon the impact of its meaning. Hopefully, these next two chapters will show how this is a confession of hope that strengthens our praise that Jesus is Lord. This is the good news.

So instead of the physical fitness analogies that I illustrate throughout the rest of the book, our theological fitness levels are going to get a workout as we go through these confessions taken from David's creed, Psalm 110. The sermon-letter to the Hebrews indeed builds a strong confession of hope for us to hold fast to in perseverance. Maybe Hebrews really is a sermon based on this psalm. Let's look at the how these same confessions of David's are taught in Hebrews. In this chapter, we will look at the first two confessions that we most certainly can hold fast to in perseverance, regarding how Jesus is Lord in his person.

## THE DOCTRINE OF THE TRINITY

This one is pulled right out of the first line of the psalm, "The LORD says to my Lord." Here we have God the Father speaking to the Son, Jesus Christ. Well, this is interesting; how does David know about a conversation between the blessed, holy Father and the Son? Preacher Charles Spurgeon marvels, "How condescending on Jehovah's part to permit a mortal ear to hear, and a human pen to record his secret converse with his co-equal Son!"[9] It is by his Spirit that this sacred discourse is revealed to David.

Reynolds also points out the role of the Holy Spirit in consecrating the Son to be David's Lord. This verse implies that there was a plan even before the creation of the world for God to call a people to himself, for the Son to accomplish the work to make this plan possible, and for the Holy Spirit to apply the Son's work to his beloved church. We call that plan the covenant of redemption, and I will discuss that in more detail in chapter 9. But think about it—as David is privy to this intratrinitarian conversation, we see that since Jesus is Lord there is nothing

9. Charles H. Spurgeon, *The Treasury of David* (Peabody, MA: Hendrickson Publishers, 1988), 2:460.

he cannot do for our salvation. And since this is planned in eternity, there is nothing we can do that will surprise God. He already knows, and he has already provided a way of grace.

We also learn about the doctrine of the Trinity in the first few verses of Hebrews.

> Long ago, at many times and in many ways, God spoke to our fathers by the prophets, but in these last days, he has spoken to us by his Son, whom he appointed heir of all things, through whom he also created the world. He is the radiance of the glory of God and the exact imprint of his nature, and he upholds the universe by the word of his power. (vv. 1–3)

Where do we even begin? What an opening hook! We see right away that Jesus the Son is the ultimate Prophet who has spoken to us. This Son is the heir of all things; therefore he must have the ultimate kingdom. As we know that the world was created by God's speech, we see here that the Son has created the world. This prophet who has spoken to us in the last days is the same one who spoke the world into existence! He sustains this very universe by the word of his power. What kind of power is this?

And what is he like? He is the radiance of the glory of God and the exact imprint of his nature. I love how Michael Reeves describes the importance of God's being as he also teaches us to delight in the Trinity, so I am going to quote him at length:

> There are two Greek words you will never use on a holiday in Corfu, but they drip with nectar. The first is *hypostasis*. I know, it sounds like a nasty skin condition, but it actually means something like "foundation" (*hypo*= "under"; *stasis*= "something which stands or exists"). . . . It is also the word used to describe God's "being"[10] in Hebrews 1:3. . . . Hypostasis describes the Father's "being," what is foundational to him.

10. Or "nature," as in the ESV quotation above.

The other word is *ekstasis*, from which we get the word *ecstasy*. It is a word to do with being beside yourself or being outside yourself (*ek*= "out from"; *stasis*= "something which stands or exists"). . . .

The Father, Son, and Spirit have their *hypostasis* in *ekstasis*. That is, God's innermost being (hypostasis) is an outgoing, loving, life-giving being. The triune God is an *ecstatic* God: he is not a God who hoards his life, but one who gives it away, as he would show in that supreme moment of his self-revelation on the cross. The Father finds his very identity in giving his life and being to the Son; and the Son images his Father in sharing his life with us through the Spirit.[11]

I got a little ahead of myself there, moving from the doctrine of the Trinity to the cross, but I wanted you to see the connection. Christ's work on the cross outflows from who he is. This is the epitome of theological fitness.

Sure, the Trinity is a difficult doctrine for us to grasp. We certainly cannot fully understand God's makeup. But Scripture teaches us that he is one being in three Persons. You can begin to see from the above quote why that matters. Stardust cannot explain the creation of beautiful, loving, thoughtful, relational, thinking human beings. We have an ecstatic God in hypostatic union. Our English translation, *being*, or *nature*, just doesn't do justice to the one God in three persons. This is most certainly a God worthy of praise!

## THE INCARNATION OF CHRIST

Also in the first verse of Psalm 110 is the phrase "my Lord." Jesus the Son is not only a Lord, but David can call him *my* Lord. This is truly amazing. Jesus descended from the line of David. Those boring genealogies that we always want to skip in our Bible reading actually labor to preserve this history. Matthew 1:1

11. Michael Reeves, *Delighting in the Trinity: An Introduction to the Christian Faith* (Downers Grove, IL: IVP Academic, 2012), 45.

begins, "The book of the genealogy of Jesus Christ, son of David, the son of Abraham." And then we pretend to pay attention until we finally get to verse sixteen about Joseph, Mary, and Jesus.

But here we have David calling his son his Lord. Incredibly, the son of David is the Son of God. Jesus, who was born in the line of David, also comes from a much "higher sonship," as Reynolds calls it. He is both David's descendant and David's Lord. Christ affirms this in Matthew 22:41–46. He gives the Pharisees a pop quiz, asking them whose son the Christ is. When they answer that the Christ is to be the son of David, he presses further by quoting Psalm 110. How could it be that his father David, while in the Spirit, calls him "Lord"? And how can he be both David's Lord and his son? Scripture tells us that the Pharisees were done asking questions after Jesus silenced them with that doozy (although Scripture says it in a much more eloquent fashion).

We can see allusions to the incarnation of Christ in the opening verses of Hebrews above, but for this section I would like to share Hebrews 2:14–16:

> Since therefore the children share in flesh and blood, he himself likewise partook of the same things, that through death he might destroy the one who has the power of death, that is, the devil, and deliver all those who through fear of death were subject to lifelong slavery. For surely it is not angels that he helps, but he helps the offspring of Abraham.

The incarnation of Christ is important to our salvation. God the Son actually condescended to a real virgin woman's womb. Her name was Mary. He descended from the line of David and was born a helpless infant just like the rest of us. The writer of Hebrews continues on from the above verses to say that Christ needed to be made like us in every way. His suffering was real. It was existential, not just some theological check that needed to be marked off on the to-do list of redemption. This portion of Hebrews then explains how the Son of God is both the merciful and faithful high priest who really could propitiate the wrath of God toward the sins of his beloved (v.17). He really can identify with us in our suffering even as he overcame temptation (v.18). We can walk by faith in the real path that Christ, the Son of God, ran before us. His perfect oblation has qualified us. As our accuser, the Devil could point to us as lawbreakers, enslaved to the dominion of sin. But Christ Jesus broke that power when he took on our flesh, wholly fulfilled the law's demands, and bore our curse.

"This is why the eternal Son became man, and as man was declared Son of God in power—it was for our sakes, because of his love for us. God's Son became like us, so that we might become like him in the resurrection."[12] What an amazing God we serve! Jesus is Lord indeed. He is the Son of God, the second person of the Trinity, and in effect of his incarnation, fully God and fully man. He is worthy of our praise for who he is.

## GOING THE EXTRA MILE

1. At what times of your life has your faith been most challenged? How did you respond? What did you cling to?

2. Where do you think you stand in the theological milk-to-meat chart? How has your level of theological knowledge helped or hindered your perseverance?

3. Does your church use any catechisms or creeds to teach you about the Christian faith? If so, which ones does it use and how are they helpful? If not, how would you articulate what your church believes about God, man, and salvation? Can you explain to others what the statement "Jesus is Lord" means?

4. How do you think learning about God's Trinitarian nature affects the way we think of him as our Creator, Savior, and Sustainer?

12. Phillips, *Hebrews*, 35.

5. Hebrews 2:7–9 also touches on the incarnation. In referencing Psalm 8:4–6, the pastor to the Hebrews is proclaiming that Jesus was made even lower than the angels. Think about that. The angels are messengers of God; they serve him. But Christ came to serve us! If angels delivered a message to us, we would think it to be pretty important. What does our final Messenger indicate about the value of the message? Do you affirm the sufficiency of God's Word revealed to us in Scripture, or do you find yourself looking for outside revelations?

6. Of all the psalms, why do you think Psalm 110 is the most quoted in the New Testament?

## | 6 |

# JESUS IS LORD IN HIS WORK

"But who do you say that I am?" Jesus had just asked his disciples to tell him what people were saying about who he was. Of course, he already knew that many people were thinking he was just another prophet, maybe even Elijah or John the Baptist. But he was preparing his disciples to be confronted with the same question (see Matt. 16:13–17). It is a very important question for each one of us to answer. Our assurance to persevere rests on who Jesus is and what he has done for us. This is why the preacher to the Hebrews exhorts us to hold fast to this confession.

Even now, we are bombarded with many false teachings about Jesus' person and his work. Kevin DeYoung gives a few suggestions of the different versions of Jesus and his work that we are faced with today:

> There's Republican Jesus who is against tax increases and activists judges, for family values and owning firearms.
>
> There's Democrat Jesus who is against Wall Street and Walmart, and for reducing our carbon footprint and spending other people's money.
>
> There's Therapist Jesus who helps us cope with life's problems, heals our past, tells us how valuable we are and not to be so hard on ourselves.

There's Starbucks Jesus who drinks fair trade coffee, loves spiritual conversations, drives a hybrid and goes to film festivals.[1]

DeYoung goes on from there, but you see his point. Can we distinguish these Jesuses from "the Christ, the Son of the Living God" (Matt. 16:16)? As passionate as we may feel about some of the above causes, these versions of Jesus are too weak. They are unable to save. Rather, they are different strategies for us to save ourselves.

Let's get back to the confessions in David's creed in Psalm 110 so that we can examine what Jesus has done and is doing for his glory and the salvation of his people. We left off looking at the first two confessions about how Jesus is Lord in his person; now we will exalt him as Lord in his work. While we champion Christ for his great strength and victory, Puritan Edward Reynolds was sure to note important confessions from this psalm regarding Christ's work.

## THE SUFFERINGS OF CHRIST

Christ's office as priest, as citied in Psalm 110:4, is connected to his suffering. Not only is he our great High Priest, but he is also the sacrifice. And his sacrifice was made complete by his suffering (Heb. 2:10). Of course we are well aware of the suffering of Christ, but Hebrews elaborately demonstrates how Jesus fulfilled every jot and tittle of the Old Testament sacrificial system. The beginning of verse 7 from our psalm says, "He will drink from the brook by the way." Christ's passion as a priest to offer himself up "once for all at the end of the ages to put away sin by the sacrifice of himself" (Heb. 9:26) was marked by bitterness and suffering. Unlike Gideon's men, who

---

1. Kevin DeYoung, "Who Do You Say That I Am?", *DeYoung, Restless, and Reformed* (blog), The Gospel Coalition, November 20, 2014, http://www.the gospelcoalition.org/blogs/kevindeyoung/2014/11/20/who-do-you-say-i-am/.

lapped refreshment from a clear brook, our Lord was to drink sorrow, death, and the very wrath of God on the path pressing to the victory.[2] It was our sin that caused his sufferings. And so John Prideaux meditates on what exactly Christ drank from the brook:

> *Mortality* by his incarnation . . . strictness and *hardness* in all his passage, by voluntary wants and poverty . . . the *strong potion of the law*, by his exact obedience and subjection . . . the *Jews' malice*, by their continual indignities . . . the *floods of Belial*, by apparent and unknown temptations . . . the *harvest wrath* of his Father, by his unspeakable agony and bloody sweat in the garden. And last of all, *of death itself* on the cross, by his sad and extreme passion.[3]

Only the Christ had the fitness to drink such a cup. And we learn from Hebrews that, just as the animal sacrifices were burned outside the camp, Jesus also suffered outside the city gate, placed with the filth and the cursed. What an encouragement to the believing Hebrews that, in order to persevere, they too needed to step outside the camp of the old sacrificial system, where they could partake in true worship due to the once-and-for-all sacrifice of the Lord Jesus Christ. Those who were still turning to the types and shadows had no right to the spiritual offering of Christ, the true sustenance and nourishment to our souls (Heb. 13:10–13).

This is an important part of our confession indeed. In fact, we are reminded of Christ's suffering on our behalf every time that we are served the Lord's Supper. Through his blood we are healed. His body, given to us, nourishes our souls. We may be quick to proclaim a Jesus who gets behind our good causes, but this means of grace reminds us how evil our own sin is. Our

2. See Fountain Elwin, quoted in Charles H. Spurgeon, *The Treasury of David* (Peabody, MA: Hendrickson Publishers, 1988), 2:477.

3. John Prideaux, quoted in ibid.

Savior was cursed because of *us*, not only for the injustice in our midst. Are we as fervent to proclaim a bloody Savior? And if we identify ourselves with him, are we also willing to carry our own cross in his path?

## CHRIST'S COMPLETED WORK AND RESURRECTION

Psalm 110 ends, "Therefore he will lift up his head." Jesus Christ is exalted and vindicated, earning victory not only for himself, but also for all those whom the Father has given him. He has not lost one. The Bridegroom is triumphant for his church. He has purchased our redemption by his blood. In Hebrews 9 we learn that Christ entered the heavenly sanctuary as our High Priest "once and for all into the holy places, not by means of the blood of goats and calves but by means of his own blood, thus securing an eternal redemption" (v. 12).

Do you know what this means? It means everything concerning our approach to God. Because of the merits of Christ's blood, the preacher to the Hebrews explains that we can now confidently enter the heavenly sanctuary:

> And since we have a great high priest over the house of God,
> let us draw near with a true heart in full assurance of faith,
> with our hearts sprinkled clean from an evil conscience and
> our bodies washed with pure water. (10:21–22)

Christ's completed work, proven by his resurrection, gives us assurance of faith. The Old Testament sacrifices pointed to this climactic event in history.

Also because of this finished work, the Hebrew recipients were given this beautiful benediction at the end of the sermon-letter:

> Now may the God of peace who brought again from the dead
> our Lord Jesus, the great shepherd of the sheep, by the blood

of the eternal covenant, equip you with everything good that you may do his will, working in us that which is pleasing in his sight, through Jesus Christ, to whom be glory forever and ever. Amen. (13:20–21)

Amen! Think about this—because of the completed work of Christ, the preacher to the Hebrews can now pray for the church to receive all the applied benefits of the theology he just taught them in detail. Because of what Jesus has done, we will bear the fruit. His work was to fulfill the oath of God, qualifying his people to be consecrated to him. God is glorified by the work of Christ transforming us into his likeness.

## ASCENSION AND INTERCESSION

Although Psalm 110 has only seven verses, we see the repeated affirmation in verses 1 and 5 that Christ is seated at the right hand of the Father. This is obviously important and meaningful. Hebrews also repeats this point, referring to this Scripture five times (1:3, 13; 8:1; 10:12; 12:2). Sitting is a position of rest. There were no chairs in the tabernacle for the Jewish high priest. Unlike the Levitical priests, who could never sit because their work was never done, Christ is now with his Father seated in a place of honor. Here he is continually making intercession for his bride. And unlike the Levitical priesthood that was interrupted by death, constantly needing successors, Christ's death was part of his priestly duty, whereby he laid down his life and took it up again. He holds his priesthood permanently, and therefore we can draw near to God in him.

> The former priests were many in number, because they were prevented by death from continuing in office, but he holds his priesthood permanently, because he continues forever. Consequently, he is able to save to the uttermost those who draw near to God through him, since he always lives to make intercession for them. (7:23–25)

What a comfort it is for the Christian to have a Mediator who continually intercedes to the holy God on their behalf! We have an unremitting advocate in the Son.

## A HOLY CATHOLIC CHURCH[4] AND COMMUNION OF THE SAINTS

In the second and third verses of our psalm we read,

> The LORD sends forth from Zion
>> your mighty scepter.
>> Rule in the midst of your enemies!
> Your people will offer themselves freely
>> on the day of your power,
>> in holy garments;
> from the womb of the morning,
>> the dew of your youth will be yours.

Here we see the images of a kingdom, particularly Christ's rule over his spiritual kingdom, the church.

In the midst of his enemies, Christ is expanding his kingdom. In fact, we too were once his enemies, but have been pierced by the living and active Word of God (Heb. 4:12). Through the preached Word, he has given us eyes to see the irresistible grace of our great and mighty king, Jesus Christ.

This creation of spiritual life always amazes me. I have a very modest garden in the spring and summer. It's exciting when my tomato plants begin to bloom. I find myself spending more time with them, just watching for the bloom to turn into a green tomato. But I always miss it. How does that happen? One evening I'm examining and watering my little blooming plants, and bam, the very next morning there's a substantial piece of fruit on the vine. That's what I think about when I read this verse about the assembly of Christ's willing warriors who

4. In case you are wondering, *Catholic* here is referring to the "universal" church, not the Roman Catholic Church.

serve as his ambassadors of good news. They appear like the morning dew. Yes, there are many who are still asleep. Their eyes cannot see the sparkle of the innumerable morning dewdrops, the growing kingdom of Christ.

Christ has inaugurated this redemptive kingdom. And until he brings in the full number of those the Father has given him, we see that this is not yet a kingdom of glory, but a kingdom of the cross. This is exactly why we need continuous encouragement to persevere in the faith. As we look forward to the city that is to come, we now live in a world that is suffering from the curse of sin. And although we have been delivered from the reign of sin, we still struggle with it every day. It is a great tension to live in between what theologians call the "already" and the "not yet" of our salvation. So the preacher emphatically exhorts us,

> And let us consider how to stir up one another to love and good works, not neglecting to meet together, as is the habit of some, but encouraging one another, and all the more as you see the Day drawing near. (10:24–25)

This is imperative to theological fitness, as we have seen from part 1.

## THE LAST JUDGMENT AND DAY OF HIS WRATH

Those who do not think it prudent to discuss the judgment and wrath of God would certainly not confess David's creed. We see in the very first verse God the Father telling the Son, "Sit at my right hand, until I make your enemies your footstool." Again, in verses 5 and 6,

> The Lord is at your right hand;
>     he will shatter kings on the day of his wrath.
> He will execute judgment among the nations,
>     filling them with corpses;

he will shatter chiefs
over the wide earth.

Our God is just. Therefore the mercy that he shows toward his people is through the righteousness of Jesus Christ. The whole Old Testament sacrificial system alluded to the fact that a mediator between our holy God and sinful man is necessary. Sinful human beings cannot approach the Holy Father clothed in their own self-righteousness.

And although these sacrificial systems were done away with, we still need to be concerned about our approach to God. We still need a mediator. In fact, they were done away with because Jesus Christ is the Mediator of a new covenant, his blood effectually atoning for our sin. The sins of all those covered by his blood in the covenant of grace were atoned for some two thousand years ago on the cross. But those who have not repented and do not trust in Christ's work over their own have a judgment day to come.

Hebrews delivers very strong warnings for those who have visibly participated in the covenant of grace and partaken of its blessings of the preached Word and the sacraments, but who show evidence that they never were one of God's children by turning away in apostasy. The wrath of God for this presumptuous group is something to fear.

> For if we go on sinning deliberately after receiving the knowledge of the truth, there no longer remains a sacrifice for sins, but a fearful expectation of judgment, and a fury of fire that will consume the adversaries. . . . How much worse punishment, do you think, will be deserved by the one who has spurned the Son of God, and has profaned the blood of the covenant by which he was sanctified, and has outraged the Spirit of grace? For we know him who said, "Vengeance is mine; I will repay." And again, "The Lord will judge his people." It is a fearful thing to fall into the hands of the living God. (10:26–27, 29–31)

In the next part of this book, we will see how these warnings serve as a means for God to preserve his children. They are real, all right, but we hear our Father's voice in them and therefore heed the admonition.

## THE REMISSION OF SINS

Verse 4 of Psalm 110 identifies the Lord as a priest forever. It was the responsibility of the priest to offer sacrifices for the remission of sins. As I mentioned above, not only is Jesus our great High Priest, but he is also the sacrifice. This is a major theme in Hebrews. In fact, the writer to the Hebrews quotes Psalm 110:4 repeatedly as the crux of his argument that Jesus is the eternal High Priest, appointed by the oath of God as Mediator of a better covenant that is ratified with better promises (5:6; 6:17–18, 20; 7:17, 21, 24, 28). That must be an important line, the pinnacle of the psalm.

The Hebrew recipients of this sermon-letter were tempted to return to the old covenant sacrificial system and ceremonies. After all, God instituted the Levitical priesthood. This was a very tangible way that the Hebrews thought they could be assured of their approach to God in worship. And since most agree that Hebrews was written before the fall of Jerusalem and the destruction of the temple, it seemed that these believing Jews were excluded from the practice they associated with true worship.

The writer to the Hebrews declares that there is not only a change in the priesthood, but a change in the law as well (7:12). In quoting Psalm 110:4, "The Lord has sworn and will not change his mind, you are a priest forever, after the order of Melchizedek," the preacher is pointing to a greater appointment made by the oath of God, who cannot lie. This is our confession of hope. It reveals the imperfection of the Levitical priesthood, which had to continually make sacrifices and replace each priest with a successor. Christ is a priest forever.

The Levitical priests only pointed to the Great Priest to come. Likewise, we have no record of the genealogy or lifespan of Melchizedek, which enables him to picture the eternal office of Christ. But we do have a record of Abraham presenting Melchizedek a tithe and receiving a blessing from this priest (Heb. 7:6; Gen. 14:18–20). This is quite remarkable, in that Melchizedek was both the King of Salem, which may be short for Jerusalem (see Ps. 76:2), and the priest. He typified two of the offices of our great Prophet, Priest, and King. As the great High Priest, Jesus Christ offered the perfect thanks offering and the perfect sacrifice of himself. He brought everlasting righteousness and peace to his people.

We may not be tempted to go back to the old covenant sacrificial system, but we have plenty of default saviors that we wrongly go to for penance. There is only one acceptable sacrifice for the remission of our sins. We can hold fast because we know that he is seated at the right hand of the Father, interceding on our behalf at this very moment. He is all we need and he is everything we need.

## RESURRECTION OF THE BODY

This confession takes us back to the first verse of our psalm. Our Lord is told to sit at the Father's right hand until all his enemies are put under his feet. In defending the resurrection, Paul quotes this verse while emphatically declaring that the last enemy to be destroyed is death (1 Cor. 15:25, 26). The writer of Hebrews quotes this verse as he explains the perfection of Christ's sacrifice (10:13). But what always gets me about this verse is Christ's remarkable patience and obedience. We know that Christ our Victor, after completing his work and ascending to the highest position at God's right hand, can easily destroy all his enemies in a second. And yet here we are, some two thousand years later, as he waits according to his Father's will to bring in every last believer.

There is some criticism that Hebrews does not include a strong doctrine of the resurrection. In some ways it is assumed. The writer briefly mentions the resurrection as one of the elementary doctrines that he wants to apply at a deeper level, since the foundation should already have been laid (6:1–2). And this is what he does. In fact, all of Hebrews 11 catalogs the history of God's people looking forward in faith to the day of Christ's return. The crux of the so-called "hall of faith" is that their confession of their hope results in life from death:

> Abel speaks though dead, v. 4; Noah and his family lived when the flood came, v. 7; Abraham was as good as dead and Sarah's womb was lifeless when Isaac was born, vv. 11–12; Isaac was given back to Abraham as a parable of resurrection, vv. 17–19; the firstborn of Israel were not killed, v. 28; women received back their dead and martyrs endured because they looked to the better resurrection, v. 35.[5]

He then highlights how the writer is leading to Jesus Christ, the author and finisher of their faith, as the climax to this list and the one who actually has received the promise (12:1–2 NKJV). Christ then, having suffered in obedience, has been exalted to the Father's right hand, having received life from the dead. He is the guarantor not only of those martyrs in chapter 11 of Hebrews, but of all of us who faithfully endure. He truly is perfecting for all time those who are being sanctified (10:14). In the new city that we receive, whose designer and builder is God (11:10), everything will be holy and incorruptible. I look forward to that new body that will be perfectly equipped to worship our God.

5. David M. Moffitt, quoted by Frederik Mulder in a November 26, 2011 comment on Mulder's article "No Resurrection in Hebrews? Think again!— Dr. David M. Moffitt's illuminating monograph," Resurrection Hope, November 18, 2011, http://resurrectionhope.blogspot.com/2011/11/no-resurrection-in -hebrews-think-again.html.

## LIFE EVERLASTING

Our last confession from David's creed brings us back to the pinnacle of his psalm: "The LORD has sworn and will not change his mind, you are a priest forever after the order of Melchizedek." Of course, we immediately see the importance of the word *forever*. If the Son is a priest forever, then his intervention on our behalf is eternal. But even more interesting and reassuring is what this verse reveals about the basis of this eternal priesthood. Remember, this is the Father talking to the Son, and Christ is witnessing the Father swearing an oath on his very life that this will be. The preacher to the Hebrews focuses on this oath when quoting from Psalm 110:4 in chapter 7:17–28, concluding, "For the law appoints men in their weakness as high priests, but the word of the oath, which came later than the law, appoints a Son who has been made perfect forever" (v. 28). This oath should give us complete assurance and confidence that God accepts Christ's intercession on our behalf.

Picking up on this appointed priesthood, the preacher to the Hebrews tells us, "Therefore he is the mediator of a new covenant, so that those who are called may receive the promised eternal inheritance, since a death has occurred that redeems them from the transgressions committed under the first covenant" (9:15). Our confidence to approach God and our hope to live with him eternally is not based on anything we can do to atone for our sin or to earn a relationship with him. It is fully reliant on the God who is faithful. Jesus Christ came to fulfill the oath that he made with his Father to be our mediator in the covenant of grace. "This makes Jesus the guarantor of a better covenant" (7:22). Those who trust in him are delivered from the covenant of works. Instead of hearing, "Do this and you shall live," we hear, "All this Christ has done."

I love how Steve M. Baugh summarizes how this oath is key to the message that we get out of Hebrews.

And that is assurance of your complete pardon in Christ; that by faith alone through his grace, the rich provision of our triune God for our full salvation in Jesus is guaranteed by the life of God. He has taken an oath that he will accept the Son's intervention on our behalf forever to effectively save us. . . . He brings the new covenant realities into effect by his high priestly intervention.[6]

That summarizes well all the confessions of David's creed.

## GOD IS FAITHFUL. JESUS IS LORD!

So there is the long and the short of it. A short psalm, my long confessional breakdown, and this last, short subheading that sums it up again: God is faithful. Jesus is Lord. And the Spirit applies it all to his beloved.

"Hold fast the confession of your hope without wavering, for he who promised is faithful." Why do you think we are exhorted to hold fast to our confession? Our focus verse from Hebrews highlights the relevance of our theology. Our confession of hope, "Jesus is Lord," also reveals that we are indeed holding fast to a Person, the Son of God. What we know to be true about God and his promises is vital to our perseverance in the Christian faith. By the time the preacher to the Hebrews exhorts us to hold fast the confession of our hope, he is confident that he has given us the *what* that we are to believe and the *why* we are to believe it, because he has faithfully preached the *Who* that is our crown of glory.

Every Christian will persevere, but we all need biblical encouragement along the way. Whatever stage of the race we may find ourselves in, it's the truth of the gospel and the power of the Spirit that will help us to endure. Sometimes we just need

6. S. M. Baugh, "Hebrews 7:18–28: S. M. Baugh," interview by R. Scott Clark, *Office Hours*, Westminster Seminary California, podcast audio, March 4, 2013, http://wscal.edu/resource-center/resource/hebrews-7-baugh.

to be encouraged to endure the mundane. Other times we will be faced with unbearable tragedy. In this world that is cursed by the effects of sin, we will encounter misfortunes such as the loss of loved ones, betrayal, persecution, illness, or rejection. We react to these circumstances according to our beliefs. This is why it is so important for us to be solid in our theology. The more that we learn about God, the stronger our faith and gratefulness grow. What is your hope?

## GOING THE EXTRA MILE

1. Why did Christ have to suffer? Look for answers in Hebrews and elsewhere in Scripture.

2. In what ways do we sometimes behave as if Christ's work on the cross weren't complete? Why is our theology important here?

3. How does the affirmation that Christ is sitting at the right hand of the Father interceding affect the way that we pray?

4. How does your theology of Christ's covenant community influence the way that you may worship? How would it affect your everyday life outside of the church?

5. Maybe, as Protestants, we don't talk about the priesthood enough. Why is this an important office to learn about? How does the book of Hebrews help us to understand this better? What does it teach us about God?

6. Read Hebrews 13:20. How does this benediction summarize some of our confessions from Psalm 110?

# PART 4

# "WITHOUT WAVERING"

# THEOLOGICAL FITNESS DO "YES," OR THEOLOGICAL FITNESS DO "NO"

I've heard it said that there are warnings, and then there are the warnings in Hebrews. Just this small admonition in our key verse to hold fast *without wavering* is a doozy!

Some of my workout routines demand numerous isometric holds. Have you tried suspending a weight or holding a strength or balance pose for sixty seconds? All of a sudden, one meager minute seems neverending. In the middle of these strength exercises my fitness instructor will yell out, "Don't fidget!" For whatever reason (um, I think it's pain!), I begin to think of a million reasons why I need to fidget. My bangs will be in my eyes, I'll have an itch on my nose, or I just simply need to squirm enough to distract me from the very uncomfortable burn. In our Hebrews 10:23 verse we see the writer also authoritatively admonishing us not to waver. In Hebrews chapter 12, we are even encouraged to endure under divine chastisement.

In this chapter we will talk about the sin that ensnares us, as well as the family mark of divine discipline. We are warned to avoid the two dangers of despising and despairing under this chastening and are exhorted to look to the source of these trials instead. As Arthur Pink put it so well, "The best of God's children *need* chastisement."[1] It is actually an outworking of God's covenant-faithfulness.

Let's face it: discipline stinks. Our children illustrate all too well this truth that we learn to cleverly disguise as adults. No one asks for discipline. And yet loving parents know that it is necessary for growth. Our Father in heaven also disciplines every one of his children. And so we are encouraged in Hebrews not only to expect divine chastisement, but also not to grow weary from it, because it is a sign of God's love. "My son, do not regard lightly the discipline of the Lord, nor be weary when reproved by him. For the Lord disciplines the one he loves, and chastises every son whom he receives" (12:5–6). He is merely repeating Proverbs 3:11–12 and themes from Job 5:17; Psalm 94:12; 119:67, 75; Revelation 3:19.[2] Hmm—since this is mentioned so many times in Scripture, it must be important and we must have a hard time remembering it!

I was just praying this morning, struggling and repenting over a particular sin in my life and asking God to help me to seek his glory in all things. I could feel myself holding back as I prayed these words. I caught myself feeding the ludicrous thought that if I really ask for this and mean it, God may give me something that I really don't want. I thought, maybe I shouldn't give God so much license to work in my life for his glory. Maybe I should be more specific on how I want him to do this. Thankfully, my bad theology radar started blasting. I found myself having to repent again over the thoughts I was having as I was repenting! First of all, God is sovereignly in control of my whole life, not just of my specific requests. And secondly, God isn't vindictive in his providence; rather, his will is lovingly bringing forth his glory and the good of his people.

1. Arthur W. Pink, *An Exposition of Hebrews* (Grand Rapids: Baker, 2004), 942. Much by way of the ideas in this chapter are reflections from Pink's commentary on Hebrews 12.
2. See cross references on Hebrews 12:5–6 in *The Reformation Study Bible ESV* (The Holy Bible, *English Standard Version*®), copyright 2005 by Ligonier Ministries.

The picture that we have of our own sanctification is far different from reality. We often have a tendency to think we are much farther along the path to holiness than we actually are. In fact, we are frequently deceived about what that path even is. While we examine our own growth in virtues and obedience, God graciously interrupts our delusional assessments with a dose of gospel truth. God's mercy does not lower the bar for our obedience, but it actually guarantees our growth in grace as we look to his holy Son, Jesus Christ. When our Father disciplines us, he is lovingly interrupting to force us to see our sin for what it really is and to recognize our own depravity and our true offense against him. It always leads us to Christ, who went before us.

Sometimes we know exactly why we are in a trial. We knew we were sinning all along, and we were just hoping it wouldn't catch up with us. It's just a matter of paying the consequences for our actions. But other times, we may be the victims. There may not be a particular offense that we have committed that can be directly linked to our suffering. And then we are left wondering why God is allowing this kind of affliction in our lives. Of course, the preacher to the Hebrews points out that Jesus is the one who actually got what we really deserve, so that we will not become weary or fainthearted in our sin (12:3). We deserve the wrath of God in hell for eternity over our sin. He is the one truly offended. And since he demonstrated his love for us on the cross, we can be confident that even when we are afflicted and don't understand why, he is sovereignly working "for our good, that we may share his holiness" (12:10).

## AFTERWARD AND NEVERTHELESS

What thoughts come to your mind when I keep bringing up exercise? Duty? Guilt? Pain? How about excitement? You may or may not enjoy exercise. But even if you do, do you always? Sometimes I have to talk myself into changing my clothes and training. What am I training for? Mainly just to maintain physical fitness—stamina for an active, healthy life.

But it doesn't always feel good.

We've seen how the preacher to the Hebrews uses the analogy of a runner in a race, and then a combatant in the Grecian Games, to exhort the believer to endurance in the faith, even under divine chastisement, as laid out for us in Hebrews 12:1–11.[3] This is an uncomfortable exhortation. Verse 11 particularly lends to the opening illustration: "Now no chastening seems to be joyful for the present, but painful; nevertheless, afterward it yields the peaceable fruit of righteousness to those who have been trained by it" (NKJV).

It's tough to motivate others for learning about divine chastisement. It's not exactly the study that everyone marks on his or her calendar with a star. We may try to run from learning about chastisement and affliction just as fervently as we avoid going through it. And yet the word *afterward* in verse 11 implies that we all will encounter these trials. It is also very searching—what will our divine discipline reveal?

Arthur Pink asserts that we will be affected one way or another by divine chastisement. Whether we are better off or worse off, the *afterward* is going to reveal our spiritual condition. He pushes the reader to ask what fruits our afflictions have produced. "Have your past experiences hardened, soured, frozen you? Or have they softened, sweetened, mellowed you? Has pride been subdued, self-pleasing been mortified, patience developed? How have afflictions, chastisements, left us? What does the 'afterward' reveal?"[4]

Are you out of shape? We see from these passages that enduring trials, even divine discipline, is no passive thing. We are to be trained, or exercised, by it. Indeed, Pink explains how this word *trained* or *exercised* is borrowed from a Greek word

3. See chapters 2 and 3.
4. Pink, *Exposition of Hebrews*, 978.

that was used in the gymnastic games. "It had reference to that athlete stripping himself of his outer clothing. Thus, this word in our text is almost parallel with the 'laying aside of every weight' in v.1. If afflictions cause us to be stripped of pride, sloth, selfishness, a revengeful spirit, then 'fruit' *will be* produced."[5]

Our motivation to train under affliction is much different from mere maintenance for a healthy spiritual life. It is to yield fruit—the peaceable fruit of righteousness. And this kind of exercise can be much more painful than physical training. What are you exercising? Pink gives some suggestions: your conscience, prayer, the grace of meekness, patience, faith, hope, and love, to name a few.

Half the time when I'm physically training, I'm not even aware of all the parts of my body that are benefiting from my workout. I imagine this is also the case spiritually. But I do know that whatever is burning is being trained. If it's my lungs, I know I'm improving my cardiovascular system. If my biceps are on fire, I'm confident that I am strengthening those muscles. So under affliction, if my pride is hurting, guess what weight needs to be laid aside? I will need to exercise much prayer and meekness in doing this. It's not joyful at the present, but painful.

Nevertheless!

We are encouraged to endure because the only one with the fitness to run the race of faith and obedience is already victorious. He has made us qualified. And now, through his powerful and helping Spirit, Jesus Christ will finish the work he has begun in us. For this, we can also be thankful for the divine chastisement of our heavenly Father. He loves his people too much to let us keep running with the full weight of our sin. And since Christ his Son has already paid the price for our sin, God will be faithful to transform us into Christ's likeness.

That is a workout indeed—"to those who have been trained by it."

5. Ibid., 979.

## PRESERVATION AND PERSEVERANCE

There is an almost continuous call to perseverance found in the sermon-letter to the Hebrews. These exhortations are strong warning passages scattered throughout chapters 2:1–4; 3:12–4:13; 5:11–6:12; 10:19–39; and 12:25–29. With this book's audience of believers (the first intended audience being believing Jews), maybe you wouldn't expect such strong language as "how shall we escape if we neglect such a great salvation" (2:3) or

> For if we go on sinning deliberately after receiving the knowledge of the truth, there no longer remains a sacrifice for sins, but a fearful expectation of judgment, and a fury of fire that will consume the adversaries. (10:26–27)

What are we to make of these passages? Are believers able to lose their salvation? Is our faith secure? Where would TULIP[6] be without the "P"? And if our salvation is secure in Christ, what is the purpose of these warnings? Are they real?

The answer is yes, and yes! Thomas Schreiner has written a helpful book on this topic called *Run to Win the Prize*.[7] In it, he explains to us, "The purpose of warnings in the NT is redemptive and salvific."[8] Warnings serve an important purpose in our growth in holiness. He explains that they are like signs that keep us on track. Schreiner quotes Charles Spurgeon to explain this further:

> So God says, "My child, if you ever fall over this precipice you will be dashed to pieces." What does the child do? He says,

6. This is a popular, old acronym used to teach the Calvinistic theology of soteriology: Total depravity, Unconditional election, Limited atonement, Irresistible grace, and Perseverance of the saints.

7. Thomas R. Schreiner, *Run to Win the Prize: Perseverance in the New Testament* (Wheaton, IL: Crossway, 2010). This is the less scholarly of the two books Schreiner has written on the subject. His other book is coauthored with Ardel B. Caneday, *The Race Set Before Us: A Biblical Theology of Perseverance and Assurance* (Downers Grove, IL: IVP Academic, 2001).

8. Schreiner, *Run to Win the Prize*, 48.

"Father, keep me; hold thou me up, and I shall be safe." It leads the believer to greater dependence on God, to a holy fear and caution, because he knows that if he were to fall away he could not be renewed, and he stands far away from that great gulf, because he knows that if he were to fall into it there would be no salvation for him.[9]

I keep hammering in these two points throughout this book: every Christian will persevere; but faith is a fighting grace. These severe warnings that we find in Hebrews and throughout Scripture help to keep us from wavering from our confession of hope. When I hear, "without wavering," I am reminded to fight to hold on. I am reminded that it isn't always going to be easy; in fact, sometimes it will be very difficult. The illustration of the race in the beginning of Hebrews 12 shows us that the Christian life demands fitness. We must persevere in holiness to reach the crown. But remember what kind of fitness we are called to. Like our Hebrews 10:23 verse, Hebrews 3:14 also encourages us, "For we have come to share in Christ, if indeed we hold our original confidence firm to the end." This entails a theological fitness.

We see that we are exhorted to hold fast not only in the beginning, but also all the way to the end without wavering. This requires fitness indeed. But think about the confession of hope that we are to lay hold of. It isn't the record of our own works; it isn't the resources of our own strength to persevere. We are exhorted to lay hold of Christ's work on our behalf. I'll repeat a quote from chapter 3: "Perseverance, then, is nothing other than grasping the scandal of the cross until the day we die."[10] We persevere because God is preserving us in Christ. Period.

9. Charles Spurgeon, "Final Perseverance" (sermon no. 75, New Park Street Chapel, Southwark, London, March 23, 1856), available online at The Spurgeon Archive, accessed March 18, 2015, http://www.spurgeon.org/sermons/0075 .htm, quoted in ibid., 49.

10. Schreiner, *Run to Win the Prize*, 76.

God is faithful to preserve his own. One of the means of preservation is to call us to perseverance through warnings. Schreiner explains that we do the same thing with our children when we tell them what will happen if they play in traffic. The warning is very real and true. Because we know that it is true, we heed the warning. Through suffering, fear, and chastisement, and in the ordinary everyday life of faith and obedience, we are encouraged to hold fast to our confession. In order to do this, we need to know what our confession is.

Fitness requires conditioning, and that's what these warnings do. For this race we need to be nourished in the words of faith and to exercise ourselves toward godliness (1 Tim. 4:6–7). I'm so thankful for the theological workout provided in Hebrews. The writer exercises us with doctrinal meat and admonishes us to chew on it (5:12–14). This sermon-letter helps us to build the theological stamina that we so need in order to persevere through divine discipline and adversity without wavering. After proclaiming Christ Jesus, the Mediator of the new covenant, he warns us again: "See that you do not refuse him who is speaking. For if they did not escape when they refused him who warned them on earth, much less will we escape if we reject him who warns from heaven" (Heb. 12:25).

## BELIEVE IT OR NOT

Wavering is really a trust issue. Do we trust in God's Word? Do we really believe his promises and his faithfulness? If we do believe, we will heed these strong warnings and move ahead with a fighting faith. We will be superabundantly engaged in the supremacy of Christ over anything the world can offer. The problem is, in this age we are still weak. Our unbelieving hearts look to other things to trust in. We need these strong warnings. Our lives show a continual pattern of sin and repentance. Our sin reveals just how weak we really are, and our faith looks to Christ's strength to deliver us from this body of death (Rom. 7:24–25).

We know that God is faithful to preserve all those he has called. Although there are many who profess faith in Christ, only genuine believers will persevere to the end. Along the way, we are sadly going to see some professors of the faith stumble and never get back up. We are going to notice others who have taken a different path. And even those of us with true faith are susceptible to backsliding for a period of time.

Joel Beeke defines backsliding as "a season of increasing sin and decreasing obedience in those who profess to be Christians."[11] This is different from the regular struggle that a Christian has with sin. The key word is *struggle*. We are sick over our sin; we hate it. And so we repent with faith in the Lord to forgive us. But when Christians are backslidden, they begin to lose their will to fight their sin. They subtly lose their desire to obey. This is the danger zone in the Christian life, one that we should mark with yellow tape and warn one another to avoid at all costs. Beeke warns, "The longer one persists in backsliding, the less right one has to claim to be a true Christian (1 John 2:3–4), for repentance is the essence of true Christianity (Acts 2:38, 20:21, 26:18, 20)."[12]

You may be wondering, "What's the difference between backsliding and straight-up apostasy?" This can be very hard to determine. Now we see why the warnings are so strong. You cannot see the difference between a backslidden Christian and one who has turned away from his profession of faith because they are both living disobediently to the faith. They are not running with us. The answer is revealed in true repentance for sin. We are all susceptible to backsliding. But true faith cannot remain in the danger zone. The Holy Spirit will lead a backslidden Christian to genuine repentance.

In Hebrews we are encouraged to run the marathon that is the Christian life, and to train like a Grecian Olympic fighter,

---

11. Joel R. Beeke, *Getting Back Into the Race: The Cure for Backsliding* (Adelphi, MD: Cruciform Press, 2011), 16.
12. Ibid.

because without holiness no one will see the Lord (12:14). It is Christ who gives us peace, and our holiness is in him alone. And yet we are told to strive like a fighter for these very things. This illustrates how hard it is to hold on to our confession of hope without wavering.

## SEE TO IT

The preacher to the Hebrews gives three strong appeals to help us to strive for holiness. In verses 15–17 we read,

> See to it that no one fails to obtain the grace of God; that no "root of bitterness" springs up and causes trouble, and by it many become defiled; that no one is sexually immoral or unholy like Esau, who sold his birthright for a single meal. For you know that afterward, when he desired to inherit the blessing, he was rejected, for he found no chance to repent, though he sought it with tears.

Richard Phillips points out that those beginning words, "see to it," really denote "the pastoral care of Christians for one another. . . . The Greek word for 'see to it' is *episkopeō*, from which comes *episkopos*, one of the main New Testament words for an elder or minister."[13] Like brothers and sisters, we are to look after one another, "and in that way we are used by God for the perseverance of those that are his own."[14] So part of our striving for peace with everyone is to promote holiness in one another. We are to make sure that no one is flirting with the danger zone. How well do we strive to take care that everyone is on the right path in the race and that they are getting back up when they fall down?

We are also told to see to it that no troubling "root of bitterness" springs up among us. While that may sound very general,

13. Richard D. Phillips, *Hebrews* (Phillipsburg, NJ: P&R, 2006), 559.
14. Ibid.

the cross-references in your Bibles may reveal that the preacher is specifically expanding on Deuteronomy 29:18. This is a strong rebuke against false teaching that leads to apostasy. In our culture of tolerance, it seems that the one pointing out a false teaching can get more criticism than the person proclaiming a different gospel. This is an admonition that the church needs to take very seriously, as we see this root of lies exposed in Deuteronomy as a poisonous fruit that can bring disaster to the covenant people.

Lastly, we are warned against profaning the holy. We hear the story of Esau trading his blessed inheritance for a bowl of stew and we think we would never be so ridiculous. But we are! We are constantly tempted to pursue worldly pleasures over true spiritual blessing. We chase situational happiness over enduring joy. Just look at the state of the evangelical church today and you will see a cavalier attitude toward holiness. Above all, our key verse bids us to esteem God's promise to us. This is a call to elevate the sacred over the common. I'm not saying that the common is bad. There's nothing wrong with eating a good bowl of stew to the glory of the Lord. But in the life of Esau we see another example of misplaced trust. He looked to external means to be fulfilled. He was so sensual that even when he sought repentance it could not be found. Esau wasn't sorry for his irreverence to his covenant relationship with the Lord; he was wallowing in his own self-pity when he realized the consequences. This is a grave warning for all who profess that our hope is in the Lord to live as we are called.

### WAX ON, WAX OFF

Growing up with a garage converted into a dojo provided quite a playground for my siblings and me. How could you ever be bored with mysterious items to explore such as a bucket full of corn? Isn't everyone looking for the perfect way to strengthen their fingers and knuckles? Thrusting them into a bucket of corn will toughen them up for sure. My brother, Luke, and I entertained ourselves by handcuffing each other (remember, my dad was also in the Secret Service) to a piece of workout equipment that was just out of reach of the bucket of corn. The key to the handcuffs was buried deep in the corn. We were left to tap into our inner MacGyver skills to escape. Good times.

And now I actually think about how those creative ways to pass the time may have served as training exercises for mental fitness. Sometimes we would come up with creative methods of escape. Was there another item in our reach that we could use as a tool to fish for the key? Maybe we could somehow knock over the bucket and the key would fall into our reach amongst all that corn. Or, and this was probably my best method of mental warfare, we could cleverly manipulate our curious little sister to come and save us. It turns out that the challenges we came up with using dad's training props were great exercises in mental fitness.

We are eager to get to the status of a mature disciple, but not so willing to go through the training and discipline to get there. It's usually not as fun as handcuffing your brother to a piece of exercise equipment. And if you are the one being handcuffed, you may wonder why you ever thought this would be a good idea. That's what the character Daniel LaRusso was probably thinking during the beginning of his training in karate. Mr. Miyagi teaches us a good lesson about training without wavering in the movie *The Karate Kid*. He asks Daniel if he is ready for his first karate lesson, and Daniel responds, "I guess so." Mr. Miyagi explains that training in karate is like walking on the road: you can walk on the right side or the left side, but if you walk in the middle you will eventually get "squished just like grape." There is no wavering. "Either you karate do 'yes,' or karate do 'no.' You karate do 'guess so' . . . . [squishing noise] . . . just like grape. Understand?"[15]

Now more eager to train, Daniel finds that his first lesson leaves him looking a lot like he's doing Mr. Miyagi's chores. He is told to wash all the cars on the lot, followed by a good waxing. And he is shown specific motions: "Wax on, right hand. Wax off, left hand. . . . Breathe in through nose, out through mouth."[16] Huh? Mr. Miyagi checks on him hours later and corrects the circular motions, reminding him of the proper form. Daniel's following so-called karate lessons involve sanding the deck, painting the fence, and giving Mr. Miyagi's house a good paint.

Finally, he is fed up when Mr. Miyagi returns from fishing after Daniel has painted his whole house. He lets his instructor have it. Where's all the training he is supposed to get? He is done being Mr. Miyagi's chore boy. That's when the wise man commands him, "Daniel-san . . . show me 'sand-the-floor.'" A confused Daniel begins to bend over to do the sand-the-floor motions, but Mr. Miyagi corrects him, showing him the rehearsed and repeated motions in the air. "Now show me wax-on, wax-off . . . paint-the-fence . . . always look eye . . . paint-the-house, side, side."[17] The next thing you know, as Daniel is doing his moves, Mr. Miyagi comes at him with hard punches and kicks, accompanied with intimidating ninja noises. Amazingly, Daniel is blocking every move with the motions he learned doing Mr. Miyagi's chores.

The constant repetition involved in the daily motions of housework has served Daniel's muscle memory to be a master of defense. Amazing! And the genius Mr. Miyagi now has a spiffy, shiny place. Likewise, God trains and disciplines us in the everyday. We usually have no idea what he is up to, but we can be sure that it is for his glory and our good. We may be bored,

15. See "Training Begins," *The Karate Kid*, directed by John G. Avildsen (1984; Culver City, CA: Sony Pictures Home Entertainment, 2005), DVD.
16. Ibid.
17. Ibid., "PAINT HOUSE."

tired, or just plain beat up from enduring whatever our normal is at the time, but we should never waver in doubt of God's will for us. It is nothing less than to be conformed to the likeness of Christ, and he will have his way to get us there.

## GOING THE EXTRA MILE

1. Why is divine discipline a necessary outworking of God's covenant faithfulness? How can this truth be a means of gospel encouragement to a believer experiencing a hard trial? In hindsight, what times in your own life have you experienced God's loving discipline to preserve you on the path to righteousness?

2. What fruits have your afflictions produced?

3. How do warnings serve as a form of conditioning in theological fitness? Why don't you think it would be enough to just receive encouragement without the warnings?

4. Read the very short epistle of Jude. It's interesting how Jude also encourages a fighting faith (v. 3) that emphasizes pastoral care for one another, just as in Hebrews 12:15–17. This brief letter also stresses the dangers of false teaching in the church and profaning the holy. Why do you think these are such important exhortations in preserving believers from apostasy?

5. What wisdom do you find in Jude 22–23 that helps us to "see to it that no one fails to obtain the grace of God"? Do you take this responsibility seriously? Do you have the kind of relationships with fellow church members to notice if someone is falling into error and sin, or for them to see the same in you?

6. So, to preserve us in the great call to hold fast the confession of our hope without wavering, we have some pretty strong warnings, divine discipline, and some specific guidelines. This calls for commitment at a serious level. Without waver-

ing. Every day. Either you theological fitness do "yes," or theological fitness do "no." How can we possibly walk in the middle of the road with these kinds of incitements? Theological fitness is a way of life. Do you find this level of commitment to be too demanding? Do you think that you can persevere without constant conditioning in the Christian faith? What happens when we waver?

# | 8 |

# PLATEAU BUSTERS

Every January, a new slew of fitness videos hits the market to target everyone motivated by New Year's resolutions. I love this time of year because it's an opportunity to stock up on the new releases made by some of my favorite fitness gurus. One of the videos I purchased promised to serve as a plateau buster.[1] *Plateau* is a dreaded word in the fitness industry. You see, the body is a very adaptable specimen. When you begin a workout program, one of the first things you notice (besides the fact that you are terribly out of shape) is sore muscles. Ah yes, the morning after will bring much pain to ordinary activities such as going down stairs and even taking a seat. In a bizarre way, I like this pain because it is an indicator that my workout is in fact working. And if you have the fortitude to continue with the program, you will indeed see the results. You will lose weight (if needed) and become stronger.

But a funny thing happens. You might be inspired by the effects you are experiencing. So you really make the lifestyle changes needed to continue in physical fitness. Maybe you have a goal weight, clothing size, triglyceride count, or bench-press number to attain. Hence, you chug along doing your same workout every day, and possibly even begin eating a healthier

1. *Personal Training with Jackie: 30 Day Fast Start*, directed by Andrea Ambandos (Beverly Hills, CA: Anchor Bay, 2011), DVD.

diet. But if this continues, you will come to find that your body adapts so well to the new routine that it becomes more efficient in performing these same activities. It therefore does not need to exert as much energy as it did in the beginning. Your body hits a plateau. Maybe you are where you want to be physically when this happens. But those who care about fitness as a lifestyle are motivated to keep their bodies challenged to ever increase in their fitness potential.

I think that, mistakenly, we may look at the Christian life as though we can hit a plateau—and we think that is a good thing. In the beginning of our walk, we may have aspirations to reach a level of Christian maturity where we can shed some of the sins that shame us. There may be a few doctrines we want to nail down and some loved ones to evangelize, along with a particular setting on the moral compass that we aspire to reach. Once we get there, we think that the cruise control will set in and we can be content. But as we embark on the pilgrim's progress, we will find that sanctification is nothing like this. There is no plateau in the Christian life. We are either growing closer to Christ's likeness or we are falling away. I was reminded of this as I was reading Hebrews 5:11–14.

> About this we have much to say, and it is hard to explain, since you have become dull of hearing. For though by this time you ought to be teachers, you need someone to teach you again the basic principles of the oracles of God. You need milk, not solid food, for everyone who lives on milk is unskilled in the word of righteousness, since he is a child. But solid food is for the mature, for those who have their powers of discernment trained by constant practice to distinguish good from evil.

While this passage should incite a fearful warning to evaluate our own sanctification, I also find much comfort in the fact that we will always be growing in our knowledge of the Lord. His Word is able to provide milk for the babe in Christ, as well as strong meat for the mature. But notice how the writer uses the word *again*. The hearers of this sermon need to be retaught because their theological fitness level is moving in the wrong direction.

There is something I find pretty interesting about these verses. The preacher is admonishing the recipients of his sermon-letter for their lack of growth. He complains that he has to give them the basic principles of the faith, the milk, when they should be ready for the steak. But, as I have said earlier, this sermon-letter to the Hebrews is no stroll in the park. It is a workout in theological fitness! Apparently the early church drank much stronger milk than we do. Or this preacher is delivering a plateau buster of a sermon. If he were to serve them milk alone, there would be no growth. In order to hold fast to their confession of hope, they needed theological strength and stamina.

## EACH REPETITION COUNTS

In reality, the plateau is a bit of a myth in fitness as well. As your body adapts to your workout routine, you inevitably have to challenge yourself in new ways to maintain the level of physical fitness that your body has reached. One of the biggest ways to bust through a fitness-plateau is muscle confusion. Our muscles become accustomed to going through the same exercises, so it is good to change things up a bit. Fresh routines can challenge them in new ways, surprising the body and forcing it to adapt. This kind of training strengthens muscles and builds stamina, as your body has to work harder.

My workout DVD that promises to serve as a plateau buster is centered on a pyramid technique. In this routine there are twelve sets of exercises through which we build up repetitions. For example, the workout starts with one dumbbell push-up from your knees, transitioning into one hammer curl from your knees. Then we do two push-ups and two hammer curls. We keep going until we reach ten of each. Once that set is done, we have done fifty-five repetitions. When you first start the two-move combination, you think that it is pretty ordinary and simple. By the time you are doing eight repetitions apiece, you're hoping you can make it to the "top" of the pyramid. Ordinary moves turn into an extraordinary feat to reach your goals.

In the verses above, one of the goals in spiritual maturity is discernment. The author of Hebrews exhorts us to be trained by constant conditioning to develop this ability to discern good from evil. *Constant.* We usually use this word in a negative context, like when someone is *constantly* doing something to get on our nerves. But this translation of "constant practice" is referring to exercising a habit, a good habit. Sitting under God's Word every Sunday in the covenant community, praying corporately, receiving the sacraments, and being subject to the discipline of the church is certainly a means of constant practice through which God promises to convey the benefits of Christ's life, death, and resurrection. And hearing a plateau-buster sermon such as Hebrews is a great way to exercise our senses.

The preacher to the Hebrews is exhorting them to constant practice in the Word of God so that they will become mature and discerning. Is your mind preoccupied with the truth revealed in God's Word? Are you continually exercised by it in study, prayer, reflection, and conversation? Or do you settle with just one or two repetitions?

I can't help but think of how God shakes things up a bit for us in our life experiences. As we are engaged in these exercises, God providentially places us in situations that shock our minds and hearts, forcing us to adapt. Of course, his Spirit is with us, guiding and transforming us through this process. It is, in fact, by depending on him that we do adapt, reaching more mature spiritual fitness. It's all so awesome how God uses his Word, his Spirit, and his means of grace in worship, all to nourish us and grow us in godliness. And I don't even have to wait until the first of the year for new workouts!

## WE DON'T PEAK IN THIS LIFE

Exercise isn't just something we do to relieve stress. And spending time in God's Word isn't just some formula to find peace in our day. We are training. There is a goal, a finish line. Those old '80s karate flicks speak to a real truth. A warrior trusts in his training. We are exercising our senses so that when we are challenged, we hold fast the confession of our hope without wavering. We have rehearsed that hope over and over. We know its ins and outs. We know it blindfolded and can still dance in its motions even with an injury. We know it backwards and inside out.

Therefore, we can recognize a fraud and see the truth even when the world tries to spin it in another direction. We know truth because he knows us. And he is faithful. He has pursued us, and we cannot be persuaded to turn from his beauty. So we fight to advance in the faith. Constant training is our obsession, our privilege. And, just like Paul writes to the Philippians, we recognize that suffering has been granted to us as a gift as we persevere for the sake of Christ.[2] We suffer with joy. And in every plateau buster we grow closer to him. We are strengthened. We find endurance that is not our own. It is that of our Forerunner. There's nothing easy or stagnant about it. We sweat. He renews us. Praise God!

I am fighting for a Warrior who has already assured my victory. He paid the highest cost, robbing Satan of any collateral. He has given us our assurance to persevere. The beauty of the Christian life is that you don't peak in your twenties. Our goal isn't merely to read through the whole Bible or to reach some moral platitude. Our goal isn't to have a Christian life that looks squeaky clean to the watching world. It isn't to marry the perfect person, get the right job, or raise bragworthy children. Our goal is nothing less than to see Jesus

2. See chapter 5.

Christ face to face and eternally dwell with him in the new heaven and the new earth.

As I press on to this finish line, which is really the beginning, I know something that frees me to help others in the race. We see Jesus sharing something profound with his disciples. In Luke 13:30 he says, "And behold, some are last who will be first, and some are first who will be last." Later, when the disciples are jockeying over who gets the greatest seat of honor at the table, Jesus rebukes them. "Let the greatest among you become as the youngest, and the leader as one who serves. For who is the greater, one who reclines at the table or one who serves? Is it not the one who reclines at table? But I am among you as the one who serves" (Luke 22:26–27). Jesus' own life, death, and resurrection teach us this paradox: the last shall be first.

This is revolutionary! I'm not exercising merely to strengthen myself and leave everyone else in the dust. The assurance that Christ gives us in perseverance also encourages us not to leave any of his loved ones behind. We are free to love our neighbors because Jesus is our advocate who lavishly loves us! We don't peak in this life, so we are being trained to be others-oriented.

## PRIDE BUSTER

A plateau buster can be a major lesson in humility. As I said above, you go into the exercise thinking that these are pretty ordinary moves that you can easily pump out. But by the time you get to the eighth repetition, you're wondering if you will make it to the end. All of a sudden, each repetition of those easy hammer curls becomes a major accomplishment of an arduous feat. It's humbling to face your limits.

Aging can be the ultimate plateau buster. I'm only thirty-seven, but I already have to deal with the fact that my body just can't do things with the same ease and finesse as in my earlier days. I'll hop on a swing with my little nieces and nephews and will feel queasy. What's that all about? I tried to show off by doing a jumping dismount from the swing, and a jolt of pain surged from my feet up to my knees. When I was a girl, I would do cartwheels across my whole backyard. When I do them with my girls now, I see stars!

But this is minor compared to what my grandparents are dealing with. It has now become too taxing for my grandma to walk up the stairs. The whole family gathered at my dad's house for a Memorial Day picnic recently, and my brother wanted to show us a video of my nephew's first tournament fight. We all scuttled down to the basement television. My grandma didn't want to miss watching her great grandson's first victory, so she waited for us all to file down, and then her husband patiently helped her down each stair. When she reached the bottom, she apologized that we all had to wait for the old lady. Of course we didn't mind at all, but it was humbling for Grandma.

I'm sure you can all relate with stories of your own about how the aging process is humbling. When I see siblings struggling with taking care of an aging parent, I reflect on how we both come into this world and go out of this world with complete dependence on others. As a babe, we love it. As an adult who used to contribute to our families and to society, it is terribly humbling.

It is equally humbling to receive a spiritual plateau buster as we mature. Arthur Pink suggests that our need for spiritual chastisement actually increases with age.[3] He has an interesting comment on Hebrews 12:9. "Besides this, we have had earthly fathers who disciplined us and we respected them. Shall we not much more be subject to the Father of spirits and live?" The King James Version opens this verse with "Furthermore." Pink suggests that this is a very humbling word because the writer has already been teaching on the benefits of spiritual discipline, and yet he feels the need to continue. In fact, Pink

3. See Arthur W. Pink, *An Exposition of Hebrews* (Grand Rapids: Baker, 2004), 956–57.

shares that through his own observation and study of the Word, he sees even more of a need for divine chastisement in our aging years.

He reminds us of the eagerness and boldness that our heroes of the faith had to serve the Lord in their youth. They were aware of their inexperience and complete dependence on the Lord as they battled giants, entered blazing furnaces, and resisted temptation.

> David did not fall into his great sin till he had reached the prime of life. Lot did not transgress most grossly till he was an old man. Isaac seems to have become a glutton in his old age, and was a vessel no longer "meet for the Master's use." . . . It was after a life of walking with God, and building the ark, that Noah disgraced himself. The worst sin of Moses was committed not at the beginning but at the end of the wilderness journey. Hezekiah became puffed up with pride near the sunset of life. What warnings are these![4]

These accounts certainly confirm that God "upholds the humble and casts down the proud."[5] Our age does not guarantee theological fitness. Often as we age, we become too confident in our own resources and strength, and we need to be reminded of what we knew in our youth: we are completely dependent on Another. Thank goodness our Lord loves us enough to deliver the pride busters. As we age, he does what it takes to remind us that our life is still ever dependent on our subjection to the Father of the spirits. Humility fitness.

## EXERCISING YOUR SENSES

Have you ever lost a considerable amount of weight? Since I grew up in a fitness-oriented family, I took for granted the

4. Ibid., 957.
5. Ibid.

physical lifestyle we lived. Our garage was converted into an "exercise room." My dad used it to teach martial arts, and my mom occupied it to teach aerobics. On vacations, Dad would post a sit-up and push-up chart and we actually thought it was fun to see who could do the most. Although I very much enjoyed the active family outings, obstacle courses, and challenges some of the workouts brought, I really didn't get the whole idea of a fit life. I thought I would always be physically fit.

And then I went to college.

Let's just say that I lived the typical life of many freshman students. In my second semester I needed a physical education elective, so I returned to my roots and picked an aerobics course. Well, they make you step on the scale at the beginning and end of the semester. To my horror, I had cruised right on past the freshman fifteen, straight to the freshman twenty! I had to bust my butt working out and dieting to shed those extra twenty pounds. I didn't weigh that much again until I was five-and-a-half months pregnant.

There's something I have noticed from losing that freshman twenty, followed by the almost thirty to forty pounds I gained with each pregnancy: it is really hard to move past that image of your heavier self. Even when I shed the weight and built back some muscle tone, I still saw myself as a heavier person. It's not as though I hated looking at myself in the mirror or anything like that. I actually wasn't sure anymore what I was looking at. Fitness trainers are well aware of this problem. Often while I am doing a workout video, the trainer will encourage me to visualize my future body. At first it would make me roll my eyes, because I don't believe that some mystical change will happen due to the power of my thinking. But there is an important lesson being taught. We need to exercise our senses as well. This involves looking ahead to our goal.

Keeping with our Hebrews 5 verses on spiritual maturity, let's take a closer look at verse 14, this time using the New King

James translation: "But solid food belongs to those who are of full age, that is, those who by reason of use have their senses exercised to discern both good and evil." Have you ever thought about exercising your *senses*? How do we do that? The context of these verses indicates that it is by looking ahead. Since Jesus Christ is our eternal High Priest, we can be confident in God's promise for our sanctification and glorification. Why would the Hebrews want to look back to the ways of the old covenant when they had a Mediator who will never be replaced and a sacrifice that never needs to be repeated? Why do we keep looking back to the sin that has ensnared us when we know we have a Forerunner who has gone ahead to guarantee our victory?

We struggle with being influenced by sight. But things are not as they seem. When I look at my own spiritual condition I can get very discouraged. Yet I exercise my faith by looking away from myself, toward my future hope. This all reminds me of a very important part of the liturgy each Sunday morning. The body of Christ comes together and gives a Corporate Confession of Sin. When I speak in unison with my fellow brothers and sisters in Christ, confessing, "We are constantly in rebellion, rejecting your wise counsel, refusing to obey your commands, and seeking our own way," I feel stripped naked in front of that mirror. I know this person very well. But, by God's grace, we are pointed to Christ in the Assurance of Pardon. My pastor clothes me in gospel assurance by saying something like,

> Although hypocrites and other unregenerate men may vainly deceive themselves with false hopes and carnal presumptions of being in the favor of God, and estate of salvation (which hope of theirs shall perish): yet such as truly believe in the Lord Jesus, and love him in sincerity, endeavoring to walk in all good conscience before him, may, in this life, be certainly assured that they are in the state of grace, and may rejoice in the hope of the glory of God, which hope shall never make them ashamed. (Westminster Confession of Faith 18.1)

Diligently keeping our focus on Christ matures our faith, enabling us to discern good from evil. We exercise our senses by truly partaking of the milk, letting it digest, and burning those calories,

> lay[ing] aside every weight, and the sin which so easily ensnares us, and . . . [running] with endurance the race that is set before us, looking unto Jesus, the author and finisher of our faith, who for the joy that was set before Him endured the cross, despising the shame, and has sat down at the right hand of the throne of God. (Heb. 12:1–2)

I am encouraged to do this because I am confident that when God looks at me, he sees his beautiful Son, Jesus Christ.

## GOING THE EXTRA MILE

1. Think about your earlier years as a Christian. Are you where you expected to be spiritually at your age now? What were your expectations in anticipation of becoming a mature Christian? In what ways have these expectations changed as you have matured?

2. Have you ever considered this sermon-letter to the Hebrews as spiritual milk? What does this teach us about conditioning the spiritually immature in theological fitness?

3. Repetition is an important factor in a plateau buster. If you are honest with yourself, do you ever feel as if you are above the need for repetition of the ordinary spiritual exercises such as going to church, prayer, and studying God's Word?

4. What personal experiences have you faced in your life that, through hindsight, you recognize served as plateau busters or wake-up calls to your theological fitness?

5. If we are to persevere by holding fast the confession of our hope, how is studying God's Word like training?

6. How does increased theological fitness training affect the way we treat fellow Christians and unbelievers?

7. What are your thoughts on humility and aging? Doesn't it seem that we would need less spiritual discipline as we mature? Do you see any analogies between our physical and spiritual weaknesses as we age?

8. Is your evaluation of yourself sometimes distorted by your past sin? How does proper perspective serve as one of the best plateau busters of all?

# PART 5

# "FOR HE WHO PROMISED IS FAITHFUL"

# | 9 |

# THE WEIGHT OF EXPECTATIONS

I don't follow Ultimate Fighting Championship (UFC) fights like I used to. Back in the day when Royce Gracie was introducing the world to the wonders of Brazilian Jujitsu, my whole family would get together to watch the fights. I also remember the crazy hype when Vitor Belfort won a fight in the Octagon at nineteen years old. His punches were insane. Now the sport has exploded and the marketing spin has changed the dynamic.

Nevertheless, as I was surfing through the channels with my husband one Saturday night, we got sucked into the pre-fight interviews for UFC 152. Now thirty-five years old, Belfort was trying to make a comeback in his scheduled match with light heavyweight champion Jon "Bones" Jones.

Maybe you've heard of Jones. A couple of years ago he made the news on the day of his UFC 128 match. He and his coaches went to a park in New Jersey to meditate for a while before the fight. Upon arriving, they noticed a distressed older couple. The couple had just been robbed, and the thief had run off with the GPS from their car. Jones and his coaches ran down the thief and held him until the police arrived. It makes me laugh to think of the providential timing of a thug, an elderly couple, and a UFC fighter in the park all at once. Anyway, Jones became an instant hero. Between this awesome display of valor and his winning record, it seemed he could do no wrong. He became the first UFC fighter to get an international sponsorship with Nike. Shazam, we have a fighting hero.

And then things went a little sour. Due to an injury, Dan Henderson had to pull out of his anticipated fight with Jones in UFC 151 just nine days before the big bout. Jones was then asked to fight a challenging opponent, Chael Sonnen, in his place. Jones declined the fight. I really don't blame him. He had been training to fight Henderson. If he were going to fight his professional best against Sonnen, he would need to train amply for that. The fans were not happy. Neither was UFC president Dana White, who then had to cancel the whole event. It wasn't pretty.

Next there came the news of a DWI after Jones crashed his Bentley into a pole. His mom bailed him out of jail. Not good.

During the pre-fight interview that Matt and I were watching, Joe Rogan talked with Jones about his tarnished reputation. He had gone from being the fans' golden boy to being booed at the weigh-in for his fight against Belfort. Jones said something that shocked me. He said that he wanted to be a good example for his fans, since he's in such a high-profile position. And yet it was a relief that people don't like him as much now. Jones explained that now people know the reality that he's not perfect. This was freeing for Jones, as he felt that he could go back to focusing on doing his job.

The weight of expectations on Jones, along with the crushing disappointment of his fans, got me thinking about the weight of expectations for a Christian. When unbelievers hear that you are a Christian, they immediately begin to look for the holes in your character. This is why the gospel message is so important. If our faith is in our own morality, we may not crash a Bentley, but we are going to crumble under the microscope of the public eye. And yet we should not lower our expectations.

Jon Jones was relieved that the public now recognized that he was not perfect. And he surely is no example of whom we should aspire to be. There was only one Man who was ever perfect. And yet this is the expectation of every Christian.

We long for perfection, and we are right to look for it. Jesus Christ lived a perfectly righteous life. He was able to bear the weight of his Father's perfect expectations. That was the plan. Through Christ, the Father reconciled us to himself (2 Cor. 5:18). Not only did Christ fulfill the perfect expectations of the Father, but he also bore the full encumbrance of our sin. Imagine that—the crushing weight of our sin on the shoulders of one Man. Who could bear it? Only our holy God. And since our sin is so reprehensible, every bit of it, Christ also bore the full wrath of God in our place. He voluntarily left his blissful communion with the Father to be cursed for our sin. In exchange, by faith, we are given his righteousness.

No, I am not perfect, but that is the expectation. My faith is in Christ and his perfect work on my behalf. He is actually making me holy. Therefore, I live in light of the person I am becoming. Right now there is a bit of a wrestling match between the flesh and the Spirit (see Gal. 5:17). Like Paul, I do things that I don't want to do, and don't do things that I do want to do (Rom. 7:21–24). But I can be vulnerable to those who may be watching, as I confess and repent of my sin, because I know that I am a work in progress. There is only one person to look to for salvation, for he is God and there is no other (Isa. 45:22). This message frees me to do my work, knowing that Christ will bless my efforts.

## WHERE DOES THE EXPECTATION COME FROM?

The million-dollar question is, "How can I know this is true?" How can believers be secure that we will indeed be made perfect in our glorification? Our Hebrews 10:23 verse tells us the answer: because "he who promised is faithful." The weight of our expectation is based on the promise of God. This theme of the promise of God runs through the whole sermon-letter to the Hebrews as the preacher expounds on the new covenant we are under.

In fact, this covenant theme is woven throughout all of Scripture. The Bible itself is a covenant treaty to God's covenant people. We are in a covenant relationship with our Creator and Savior, and it is by God's faithfulness to his covenant that we can be assured that we will persevere to our glorified state in communion with him.

The language of covenants and covenant treaties is not very common today. We usually talk more in terms of promises and contracts. And unfortunately, we see a lot of those broken. Of course we know that the security of a promise depends on the one who is making the promise. And this is the beauty of an oath made by God himself. But what exactly is this promise, when did God make it, and whom did he make it with? These are the questions that covenant theology answers.

## COVENANT TREATY

When Moses wrote the Pentateuch, the Israelites would have had an understanding of Near Eastern covenant treaties. The mightier ruler,[1] or suzerain, would make a covenant with a lesser ruler, or vassal, and establish a treaty articulating the sanctions of the covenant, along with its curses and blessings. It would typically begin with a preamble, or a history of this mighty ruler and his works. Michael Horton explains how, in our day, a covenant establishes a constitution, much as Near Eastern covenants established a treaty, and how even the constitution of the United States of America begins with a preamble: "We the people . . ." He then points out the preamble language in Genesis, "In the beginning, God . . ."[2]

---

1. See Michael Horton, *The Christian Faith: A Systematic Theology for Pilgrims on the Way* (Grand Rapids: Zondervan, 2011), 151–55.
2. Ibid., 152.

So God was inspiring Moses to write in a manner that his people clearly understood as covenant language. God is the mighty King who had delivered his people from Egypt, and this covenant treaty was going to identify him more clearly to his people and further define their relationship.

But God wasn't borrowing from Near Eastern culture when he established a covenant through Moses or had him record a covenantal history with his people. Louis Berkhof highlights,

> Quite the opposite is true; the archetype of all covenant life is found in the Trinitarian being of God, and what is seen among men is but a faint copy (ectype) of this. God so ordered the life of man that the covenant idea should develop there as one of the pillars of social life, and after it so developed, He formally introduced it as an expression of the existing relation between Himself and man.[3]

And so, even today, we enter into covenants such as marriage and operate as a society under a constitution.

Promise is part of God's character. God's words are promise, and he is faithful to himself. He exists as one being in three persons, a beautiful congruency of diverse unity. The persons of the Father, Son, and Holy Spirit harmonize in God's being in a way that we can only imagine. And this perfect relationship that exists within the Trinity contains no deception. When God makes a promise, every piece of it is true and can be counted on. And in his grace, God did not just make promises; he faithfully recorded them to establish his covenantal relationship with his people. We can learn about God through the covenants he has made. Covenant theology teaches us about God's relationship with his people through the promises he has made. A better understanding of the covenants God has made with his people

3. Louis Berkhof, *Systematic Theology*, new combined ed. (Grand Rapids: Eerdmans, 1996), 263.

gives a better understanding of Scripture and the character of God himself.

As we are examining the weight of our Christian expectation with its basis in the promise of God, I am going to use a fitness strategy called supersets. A superset technique can be used to work the same muscle group with back-to-back exercises. The different consecutive movements will work out each angle of the muscle before you take a rest period. (Our "official" rest period is coming in chapter 10!) Let's do a little mental/theological fitness workout by hitting that brain muscle with three different angles of what covenant theology teaches about God.

## GOD IS THE MIGHTY SUZERAIN

The promise-maker of a covenant shoulders a position of authority. Although you see substantial covenants woven throughout Scripture,[4] there are three overarching covenants. My supersets hit these three: the covenant of redemption, the covenant of works, and the covenant of grace. From this very first covenant of redemption made before the beginning of time, we will see that God is the mighty King and we are the vassals. He is the promise-maker and we are the recipients. All of God's covenants with his people stem from the covenant of redemption that was made between the persons of the Trinity.

The covenant of redemption is distinct from the other covenants in that it was made before time began between the persons of the Trinity. God makes an intratrinitarian promise to himself to give the Son a bride. But like all other covenants, there is a pattern of obedience and reward. Christ voluntarily promises to earn his reward and ours by securing our redemp-

4. The covenant of redemption, the covenant of works, the covenant of grace, the new covenant, and God's covenants with Noah, Abraham, Moses, and David.

tion. And likewise, the Holy Spirit promises to apply Christ's earnings to his people. The Westminster Confession of Faith (WCF) teaches,

> It pleased God, in his eternal purpose, to choose and ordain the Lord Jesus, his only begotten Son, to be the Mediator between God and man, the Prophet, Priest, and King, the Head and Savior of his church, the Heir of all things, and Judge of the world: unto whom he did from all eternity give a people, to be his seed, and to be by him in time redeemed, called, justified, sanctified, and glorified. (WCF 8.1)

We see in this great covenant a loving God who seeks us out for himself to lavish us with Christ's own inheritance. Our weight of expectation is "he who has promised" before time.

Scripture is peppered with references to this intratrinitarian covenant, but we see a glimpse of it in our Psalm 110 verses that are taught so well in Hebrews. In Psalm 110:4, we read about God's covenantal oath to his Son: "The LORD has sworn and will not change his mind, you are a priest forever after the order of Melchizedek." Amazingly, David is recording part of an intratrinitarian conversation. When did the Father swear this oath to the Son? The oath promises that Christ is a priest *forever*, which indicates an eternal oath.

What is the need for an eternal priest in the order of Melchizedek? This covenant of redemption shows us the direction of our perseverance. If you remember from chapter 5, this is part of David's creed: life everlasting. This is what the preacher to the Hebrews is expounding. The believing Hebrews were well aware of the fact that they needed a mediator. But they were tempted to return to the traditional confidence of a mediator from the priestly line of Levi. We see from David's creed in Psalm 110 that a greater priest has been appointed. In the tribe of Levi, the priests always needed to be replaced. This can't be God's eternal destination for his people. Like Melchizedek, Jesus Christ is both a king and a priest. The Hebrews needed to see that God himself appointed Jesus as a priest forever with an oath.

> Now if perfection had been attainable through the Levitical priesthood (for under it people received the law), what further need would there have been for another priest to arise after the order of Melchizedek, rather than one named after the order of Aaron? For when there is a change in the priesthood, there is necessarily a change in the law as well. (Heb. 7:11–12)

The old covenant that required mediators through the tribe of Levi was not lasting. It was meant to point to the true Mediator who was chosen in eternity. The Hebrews knew of their need, but they were tempted to trust in a system that was now fulfilled by another. "But as it is, Christ has obtained a ministry that is as much more excellent than the old as the covenant he mediates is better, since it is enacted on better promises" (8:6).

God is the mighty Suzerain, and his eternal Word stands. He cannot break a promise he made to himself, and he swore by an oath to send his Son as our priestly sacrifice. Think of what this means for our expectation. We do not expect to send a priest once a year into the Holy of Holies to atone for our sin.

> But when Christ appeared as a high priest of the good things that have come, then through the greater and more perfect tent (not made with hands, that is, not of this creation) he entered once for all into the holy places, not by means of the blood of goats and calves but by means of his own blood, thus securing an eternal redemption. (Heb. 9:11–12)

The covenant of redemption is the eternal promise made between the persons of the Trinity, which guaranteed that out of all the Father has given to the Son, he would not lose one. Jesus' High Priestly Prayer recorded in John 17 also refers to this covenant. Here we see Christ talking about the people

164

who the Father gave him, his being sent by the Father, and his return to the Father in glory. And he sums up the endgame with, "Father, I desire that they also, whom you have given me, may be with me where I am, to see my glory that you have given me because you loved me before the foundation of the world" (v. 24). How does Jesus know about all this? He is referring to the oath that his Father made in love before the foundation of the world. And now that he has ascended to the right hand of the Father making intercession for his people, he has sealed us with his Spirit as a guarantee that his work is effectual for our salvation. God said it, Christ did it, his Holy Spirit is applying it, and we can count on it.

The Hebrews understood their need for a mediator because of another covenant God made with his people. This covenant taught them something very important.

## THERE ARE SERIOUS REQUIREMENTS TO HAVE A RIGHT RELATIONSHIP WITH GOD

Covenant theology teaches us what it takes to have a right relationship with God. We see the language of covenant in the beginning of Genesis, and we are immediately introduced to the covenant of works. To begin with, God is identified as Adam's creator who made Adam and Eve in his own image. This is important, as we already see an ontological difference between the Creator and the created. God is not a created being. No one or no thing made God; he is an eternal being. And so there is a voluntary condescension on God's part for him to establish a covenantal relationship with Adam.

> The distance between God and the creature is so great, that although reasonable creatures do owe obedience unto him as their Creator, yet they could never have any fruition of him as their blessedness and reward, but by some voluntary conde-scension on God's part, which he hath been pleased to express by way of covenant. (WCF 7.1)

God was pleased to condescend to communicate with man by establishing a covenant with him. Created in the image of God, Adam was given life and land with a purpose: to image his creator. Adam and Eve were created to live in the presence of God, sinless, in a holy land. And they were to expand God's presence as they were fruitfully multiplying their family, cultivating the land, and building culture. Adam was given the kingly task of dominion as well as the priestly task of guarding the garden temple of Eden as they glorified God for all he had given them.

God promised eternal life to Adam and Eve, with the condition of their obedience. "The first covenant made with man was a covenant of works, wherein life was promised to Adam; and in him to his posterity, upon condition of perfect and personal obedience" (WCF 7.2).

The stipulation that he gave them was that they could eat from any tree in the garden except for the tree of the knowledge of good and evil. Adam's obedience would earn eternal life not only for himself, but for all mankind as well. His disobedience would bring a curse of death. "In the day you eat of it, you shall surely die" (Gen. 2:17). Of course, we know what God meant when he said this. Adam and Eve did not drop dead when they first partook of the forbidden fruit. But they immediately began the process of physical death, and their spiritual state was even more detrimental. No longer could they approach God in their own righteousness. Sin had contaminated their entire being, and they were now unholy. Without a mediator, they had no hope for a right relationship with God.

Even worse, Adam did not merely represent himself and his own relationship with God. He represented all mankind in his disobedience. Their spiritual nature as "dead in trespasses and sins" would be passed down to all humanity.

The covenant God made with Adam and his posterity was familiar to the Israelites after the Sinai covenant. We see God's moral law affirmed in the Ten Commandments, engraved on stone. But this time the law was given as a dispensation of God's grace, disclosing all his righteous requirements on Mount Sinai after he had first rescued the Israelites from slavery in the land of Egypt, and then accordingly giving them direction on how to live a holy life (see Ex. 19:3–6). In this revelation of God's law, we find not only his holiness but our own bankruptcy. The Israelites were unable to fulfill the law, and neither are we.

The preacher to the Hebrews passionately explains that believers are now under a different kind of covenant altogether. In fact, the covenant of works pointed to the covenant of grace. Our Mediator, Jesus Christ, has perfectly fulfilled the covenant of works. No one in the history of God's people was ever saved through that covenant, but by looking to the future Messiah who was to fulfill it. Even Moses, who delivered this covenant to the people on Mount Sinai, was employed for Jesus.

When a covenant is made, there are often public rituals of ratification. This usually involves the shedding of blood. The act is actually called "cutting a covenant,"[5] and the shedding of blood represents the curse that will come upon the one who breaks the covenant. We see this in the Sinai covenant when the vassals, God's people, swear to keep the covenant sanctions. They proclaim, "All the words that the LORD has spoken we will do" (Ex. 24:3), while Moses sprinkles the blood from the offerings on both the altar and the people, saying, "Behold the blood of the covenant that the LORD has made with you in accordance with all these words" (Ex. 24:8).

The Israelites were terrified as they saw God's power manifest itself on Mount Sinai with pounding thunder, jolting lightning, smoke, and trumpet sounds. Of course they wanted to be in a right relationship with this holy, powerful God by doing

5. See Horton, *Covenant and Salvation*, 16. He also notes, "Dennis J. McCarthy, S.J., points out that 'to cut a covenant' is used as early as the 1400s BCE in Aramaic and Phoenecian as well as Hebrew records" (Dennis J. McCarthy, S.J., *Treaty and Covenant: A Study in the Ancient Oriental Documents and in the Old Testament* [Rome: Biblical Institute Press, 1963], 52–55, quoted in ibid.).

his will. But the law only condemned them. Sure, the law was good, but it didn't come with the power for one to fulfill it. No matter how badly God's people wanted to obey, or even with good intentions thought they might be able to obey as they experienced the holiness of God, their sinful nature just couldn't follow through.

This is our condition without Christ. We may know the law, and we may see that the law is good, but since we are all in Adam, the reign of sin so permeates our hearts, minds, and bodies that we cannot do good. We cannot earn our own salvation. We cannot fulfill the overwhelming requirements of a holy God.

This leads to the purpose of the covenant of works. From the very beginning with Adam, we see that there is no goodness other than God. Even when Adam was without sin, his goodness was dependent on obedience to God's Word, to what *God* says is good. God's law, like God himself, is perfectly righteous. But Adam did not obey even when he was capable, and the Israelites learned that they could not meet these demands no matter how urgent they knew it to be. The remnant of God's people throughout the Old Testament knew that the law was good, and it directed them to holy living. But like us, they were saved by faith.

The covenant of works can leave us in despair, asking, "How are we to be in the presence of a holy God? How are we to have a right relationship with our Creator?" Or it can lead us to the glorious answer to these questions, our third superset.

## GOD HIMSELF HAS FULFILLED THOSE REQUIREMENTS ON BEHALF OF HIS PEOPLE

Praise God that he did not stop at the covenant of works. And I've already alluded to the outworking of his covenant of grace even when he delivered his law to the Israelites on Mount Sinai.

> Man, by his fall, having made himself incapable of life by that covenant, the Lord was pleased to make a second, commonly

called the covenant of grace; wherein he freely offereth unto sinners life and salvation by Jesus Christ; requiring of them faith in him, that they may be saved, and promising to give unto all those that are ordained unto eternal life his Holy Spirit, to make them willing, and able to believe. (WCF 7.3)

Many people like to think of the Old Testament times as showcasing the wrath and judgment of God, while the New Testament is a picture of grace. But right from the beginning of Scripture we see that the two covenants of works and grace run throughout all of God's Word. God did administer the covenantal curse for breaking the covenant of works after the fall, but he also gave a promise of redemption through his Son in his second covenant of grace.

This covenant was differently administered in the time of the law, and in the time of the gospel: under the law, it was administered by promises, prophecies, sacrifices, circumcision, the paschal lamb, and other types and ordinances delivered to the people of the Jews, all foresignifying Christ to come; which were, for that time, sufficient and efficacious, through the operation of the Spirit, to instruct and build up the elect in faith in the promised Messiah, by whom they had full remission of sins, and eternal salvation; and is called the old testament. (WCF 7.5)

Under the gospel, when Christ, the substance, was exhibited, the ordinances in which this covenant is dispensed are the preaching of the Word, and the administration of the sacraments of baptism and the Lord's Supper: which, though fewer in number, and administered with more simplicity, and less outward glory, yet, in them, it is held forth in more fullness, evidence and spiritual efficacy, to all nations, both Jews and Gentiles; and is called the new testament. There are not therefore two covenants of grace, differing in substance, but one and the same, under various dispensations. (WCF 7.6)

Whereas the Israelites sprinkled the blood of the animal offerings all over themselves and the altar, acknowledging a curse for not meeting its stipulations, God sent his own Son to shed his blood once and for all, taking our curse, and applying his righteousness in grace. God foreshadows this great event even as he is announcing the curse on Adam and his posterity for his and his wife's disobedience to the covenant of works (Gen. 3:15). And we see an even greater picture of the ceremony that ratifies the covenant of grace when God formally makes his promise to Abraham.

Abram was probably part of a moon-worshiping family when the Lord called him out. God tells Abram that he will make of him a great nation and that he will make his name great. God promises, "I will bless those who bless you, and him who dishonors you I will curse, and in you all the families of the earth shall be blessed" (Gen. 12:3). Abram obeys the call out of Ur. But he and his wife are old, and despite their own strategies Sarah still has not conceived a child. How were the families of the earth to be blessed through them? Still, God affirms his covenant, telling Abram that he will have an heir and that his offspring will be as numerous as the stars in the sky (Gen. 15:5). "And he believed the LORD, and he counted it to him as righteousness" (v. 6). Abraham was justified by faith, not by works. All who are his offspring are also those justified by faith.

To ratify his promise, God had Abram bring him a heifer, a goat, and a ram and then sever them in half. More blood. God's presence then passed through these halves to affirm that the curses would fall on himself if he broke his covenant. Although we are covenant-breakers, God is a covenant-keeper. God did take the covenant curse on himself. He sent his very Son, who fulfilled all the stipulaetions of the covenant on our behalf and then shed his blood, taking the curse for our unfaithfulness. Jesus Christ is the Seed of Abraham, and all who have faith in him will not perish but have everlasting life.

Through this lens of God's promise, we can see the administration of grace even in the giving of the law on Sinai. God's covenant of grace certainly doesn't nullify his moral law. We must be holy to have eternal life with God. Thankfully, in the covenant of grace we are given Christ's holiness, and he has endured the curse due us as covenant-breakers. As Brown and Keele explain,

> The covenant of grace is the historical outworking of the covenant of redemption. . . . It was for Christ a covenant of works. . . . His obedience under this covenant is the foundation of the gospel and the covenant of grace. The covenant of grace is essentially the application to sinners of the benefits earned by Christ through his fulfillment of the covenant of redemption. In this covenant, because of Christ's obedience, God brings his people into communion with himself and promises them, "I will be your God and you will be my people." His promise is not on the basis of *their* obedience, but on the basis of *Christ's* obedience. It was works for Christ so that it is grace for us.[6]

The covenant of grace provides the expectation of our hope. There is something very important to recognize about God's dealing with his people through covenant: it is as practical as you can get. His commands demand a response of obedience or disobedience. And his promises demand his very own action: the Son of God condescending to come to earth as an infant on an actual day in history. He actually grew as we do, and was tempted as we are, though without sin. Jesus Christ really carried the weight of our sin on a tree and bore the full wrath of God poured out on our unrighteousness. Because of this, Christ's true righteousness can be applied to all who believe on him. And because of the Spirit's application of that work, we

---

6. Michael G. Brown and Zach Keele, *Sacred Bond: Covenant Theology Explored* (Grandville, MI: Reformed Fellowship, Inc., 2012), 59.

are now able to respond to God in obedience, in confidence that God is working his sanctification process in us.

The covenant of redemption wasn't just some hypothetical situation or theorizing made in heaven. It was carried out. It reveals to us who God is, who we are, and how he is glorified. All those who refuse to dwell on Mt. Zion with him for eternity insist on their own righteousness. By laboring to fulfill righteousness on their own, they will be faced with even greater horrors than Israel did on Mt. Sinai. But those of us who believe are counted as righteous, Abraham's children of faith. His Seed is our salvation.

> For you have not come to what may be touched, a blazing fire and darkness and gloom and a tempest and the sound of a trumpet and a voice whose words made the hearers beg that no further messages be spoken to them. For they could not endure the order that was given, "If even a beast touches the mountain, it shall be stoned." Indeed, so terrifying was the sight that Moses said, "I tremble with fear." But you have come to Mount Zion and the city of the living God, the heavenly Jerusalem, and to innumerable angels in festal gathering, and to the assembly of the firstborn who are enrolled in heaven, and to God, the judge of all, and to the spirits of the righteous made perfect, and to Jesus, the mediator of a new covenant, and to the sprinkled blood that speaks a better word than the blood of Abel. (Heb. 12:18–24)

Since Christianity is a historic faith based on actual events in time, we know that God has done what he has promised. God's very blood ratified his covenant. We look forward to its consummation. Christ carried the weight of expectations for his people so that we can trust that God's complete work of glorification will be done in us. Even now, Christ is expanding his kingdom through his church. He is calling people from all parts of the earth into his covenant community. And we expect him to come for his bride. Because of his promises and his fulfillment, we don't have to be anxious to live up to others' expectations. Rather, we live as changed people being formed into Christ's likeness. In gratitude for everything he has done and is doing, we really can love and serve one another as a reflection of his great love for us.

## GOING THE EXTRA MILE

1. If the weight of our expectations is based on the promise of God, what is the extent of our confession of hope for our eternal condition? Is this hard for you to believe sometimes? Explain. How does focusing on this expectation affect the way you live today?

2. How does understanding Scripture in relation to a covenant treaty affect your perspective in reading it, or in sitting under God's Word being preached?

3. How is a covenant treaty different from a love letter?

4. Do you have any issues with Adam representing all mankind in his obedience and disobedience? Explain how this federal representation for salvation actually benefits us.

5. Read Exodus 19 and 20 and consider this covenant given on Mt. Sinai. In what way or ways is this a gracious covenant?

6. Does the covenant of grace reveal any unnecessary expectations that you may be putting on yourself? Why is it important to recognize how Christ met and fulfilled every demand of the law? How can this realization help us in our own obedience?

# | *10* |

# ACTIVE REST

According to the Centers for Disease Control and Prevention and the American College of Sports Medicine (ACSM), approximately 60 percent of well-meaning people who begin a workout routine give up within the first six months.[1] And then there's a small percentage out of the 40 percent left who encounter overtraining syndrome. Monique Savin quotes an ACSM article affirming that while we know that to improve our fitness levels training must involve intensifications in our conditioning, even to the point of exhaustion, "The vast majority of this improvement occurs during the rest and recovery period after an intense training bout. The rest and recovery period is therefore extremely important for the training athlete to make improvements in fitness."[2]

Interesting. To improve our fitness levels, we need to increase our training to the very point of fatigue and then incorporate

1. The statistic refers to both men and women. See "Physical Activity and Public Health: A Recommendation from the Centers for Disease Control and Prevention and the American College of Sports Medicine," *The Journal of the American Medical Association* 273, no. 5 (February 1, 1995): 402–7, doi:10.1001/jama.1995.03520290054029, quoted in Cheryl B. Anderson, "When more is better: number of motives and reasons for quitting as correlates of physical activity in women," *Health Education Research* 18, no. 5 (October 2003): 525–37, http://her.oxfordjournals.org/content/18/5/525.full#ref-50.

2. Monique Savin, "Active Rest Personal Best: Light Exercise on non-training days makes world of difference," Sun Media, July 30, 2007, http://chealth.canoe.ca/columns.asp?columnistid=11&articleid=22156&relation_id=0.

a proper rest and recovery period. As it turns out, proper rest and recovery might not be exactly what you think. I have picked up on the benefits of active rest for physical fitness. During my day off of regular exercise routines, engaging in light, low-stress activity can be more beneficial than, say, bonding with my couch. Slightly increasing blood flow on my rest day speeds muscle recovery by more quickly flushing out lactate and other toxins from my body. For me, this is the joy and reward of fitness. I aim to train throughout the week so that I can enjoy regular life with ease. Things like taking a walk in the neighborhood, playing with the kids, or digging out my garden may raise my heart rate a little, but they are light exercise. For me, the goal of training and conditioning *is* active rest. I condition my body to have the fitness for an active life.

So what's the theological connection? Sunday and eternity. At the beginning of the week, Christians are given a day for rest and worship as a covenant community. Also known as Resurrection Day, Sunday is given to us as a foretaste of our future eschatological hope. It is modeled after creation.

## THE LORD RESTED

We are all very familiar with this pattern of creation. God created for six days, taking notice of the goodness of his work at the end of each day. After the six days, we see in Genesis, "And God saw everything that he had made, and behold, it was very good" (1:31). We read that, after he completed his work of creation, God rested on the seventh day. We also read, "So God blessed the seventh day and made it holy, because on it God rested from all his work that he had done in creation" (Gen. 2:3).

What does it mean that God rested? We know that God doesn't need to take a break. He doesn't grow weary and need refueling. First, we see that God has completed his work (2:1). This gives us confidence that our God finishes what he begins. Not only did he complete his work, but God also saw that it was very good. Think about that for a moment. Think about the beauty and harmony of God's perfect creation before sin entered the world. There was no "If only I had chosen this color for the leaves instead."

Think about the garden temple. This was a place where God could dwell with Adam and Eve. They enjoyed his presence in complete holiness. All their work was consecrated to him. Of course, our gardens now are no holy temples. But even when they are at their height of beauty, when every plant or flower is blooming at peak, when all the weeds are picked and all the mulch is laid, I still have to suffer bees, stink bugs, and mosquitoes. In order to be satisfied with my work, I have to lower the standards a bit. But not God. He was wholly pleased with his work. And this is what it means for his rest.

When we read that God rested, it certainly can't mean that he removed his hand from the work of sustaining the creation that he had just made. It means that he enjoyed it. John Calvin explains, "On the whole, this language is intended merely to express the perfection of the fabric of the world; and therefore we must not infer that God so ceased from his works as to desert them, since they only flourish and subsist in him."[3] This is what we all long for, is it not? Our hope is to dwell with our God in holiness, with a full blessing on all our work in him.

This is also the case with the first man. The original day of rest was a symbol to Adam of what he was working for, that is, a place of eternal Sabbath rest with the Father. It was on Saturday, the last day of the workweek. God consecrated the Sabbath. He made it holy, set apart for him.

After the fall, God summoned Adam and Eve and they hid. Communion with their Creator had been violently disrupted. Adam and Eve felt the shame for their sin and recognized that they could not approach their Lord in unrighteousness. Again,

---

3. John Calvin, *Calvin's Commentaries*, Vol. 1, *Genesis*, trans. John King (repr., Grand Rapids: Baker, 2003), 104.

we see another picture of the gospel when God pursued them and provided a sacrifice to cover their nakedness. God did not take away that day of rest, but the curse he delivered on all his creation affects everything that we do. Our best efforts fall completely short because of our depravity and sin, and yet God still calls us to rest.

Further revelation about rest was given when God delivered the Ten Commandments to his people. The Israelites were to remember the Sabbath and keep it holy, as they were specially set apart in a covenant relationship with God. When Moses recorded these words from God for the Israelites, they were already very familiar with this pattern of work and rest.

We know that the Pharisees went way out of hand with the whole Sabbath thing. Jesus set them straight by proclaiming that he is the Lord of the Sabbath (Mark 2:27–28). He is the Lord of rest. We learn that the Sabbath was made for man, not the other way around. But if we are to truly rest, we are to rest in Christ's goodness, Christ's work, not our own. What is your relationship with work?

## WHO'S RUNNING THE WORLD?

Even now, we find ourselves constantly striving. What are we trying to prove? What blessing are we trying to earn? With today's technology, work has seeped into every moment of our day. We are always available. As we are striving for significance, we have blurred the lines. When does work actually begin, and when does it end? Many of us check our emails before and after we go to bed, and we carry our smartphones around to alert us when we are being summoned. We are making things happen and keeping things going. The problem is, I don't run the world. It's not my striving effort that is providentially creating and maintaining all that is good.

Anyone who relies on his or her own efforts will be condemned. Isaiah 57:20 describes the restless condition of relying on one's own efforts: "But the wicked are like the tossing sea; for it cannot be quiet, and its waters toss up mire and dirt." What is the worth of our own efforts in righteousness? Again, in Isaiah 64:6 we see, "We have all become like one who is unclean, and all our righteous deeds are like a polluted garment; we all fade like a leaf, and our iniquities, like the wind, take us away." The human condition without Christ is one of total depravity. Every part of our being is affected by the covenant curse from the fall. We are utterly unable to be righteous, and therefore we are restless in a quest for validation.

But we are programmed to desire rest. Think about it—about one third of our lives is spent sleeping. We are forced to rest, even when we don't want to. We are forced to give up, close our eyes, and drift into a completely vulnerable, unconscious state. This should be a constant reminder to us of our dependent condition. We must resign.

And yet the distressed can never close their eyes for good; therefore they will never have rest. Revelation 14 explains that the wicked shall "drink of the wine of the wrath of God, which is poured out full strength into the cup of His indignation. He shall be tormented with fire and brimstone in the presence of the holy angels and in the presence of the Lamb. And the smoke of their torment ascends forever and ever; and they have no rest day or night" (10–11 NKJV). Charles Spurgeon preached about this torment:

> But what is sin to be in the next state? We have gone so far, but sin is a thing that cannot stop. We have seen whereunto it has grown, but whereunto will it grow? For it is not ripe when we die; it has to go on still; it is set going, but it has to unfold itself forever. The moment we die, the voice of justice cries, "Seal up the fountain of blood; stop the stream of forgiveness; he that is holy, let him be holy still; he that is filthy, let him be filthy still." And after that, the man goes on growing filthier and filthier still; his lust develops itself, his vice increases; all those evil passions

blaze with tenfold more fury, and, amidst the companionship of others like himself, without the restraints of grace, without the preached word, the man becomes worse and worse; and who can tell whereunto his sin may grow? ... What I am when death is held before me, that I must be forever.... Where death leaves me, judgment finds me. As I die, so shall I live eternally.[4]

How scary is that? Just as Sunday is a taste of the believer's heavenly rest in Christ, the constant restlessness of unbelievers in their own efforts is a taste of their eternal state. Here is an opportunity for us to share the good news of the gospel to those tired of struggling in their own efforts. Our own attempts at righteousness and joy always fail. In fact, those attempts are wicked. Out of love for our neighbor, we can't let them be fooled into thinking that one day they can close their eyes for good and that's it.

## REST NOW

But what the first Adam failed to accomplish for his progeny, the second Adam, Jesus Christ, secured for his people. Because of this great news, our Sabbath day is at the beginning of the week. First we rest in Christ before we are called out to labor in our secular vocations. What a great gift we have in this present world of suffering to be given Sunday, a day of rest from our labors, a taste of our eschatological hope to be fed and clothed by our Savior.

We need this constant reminder because our default setting is to strive to find significance in our own work. It is no wonder that we feel important when we get those smartphone notifications. We are summoned beings, after all. We were made to be responders. God's people are summoned to the covenant renewal ceremony, and we come to worship the One who has

4. Charles H. Spurgeon, *Spurgeon's Sermons* (Grand Rapids: Baker Books, 1999), 1:283–84.

done it all. He is wholly satisfied in Christ's work on our behalf. Sitting under the preached Word and partaking in the sacraments, we see that we are receivers. Christ's blessings are conveyed to us through these means of grace. Afterward, we are sent out with a benediction to live as we are called.

Most days we are going through the motions, trying to succeed in our everyday tasks. And yet, even though we accept and participate in the ordinary, we don't want to settle for mediocrity. We want our duties and service to be meaningful. Usually we go about this striving without much confirmation on whether or not we are excelling in our vocation.

For example, I never hear, "Way to get that toothpaste out of the sink, Mom!" or, "I really appreciate how you made me do that for myself. I see the wisdom there in how you are preparing me for adulthood." Nope, I'll never hear that one. However, we do occasionally have those beautiful moments when we are encouraged that we are doing well where the Lord has placed us. There are a handful of times that I have really felt validation in my life:

- when I received my National Teacher's Examination (NTE) test scores.
- when I was critiqued by art and creative writing professors
- when my husband asked me to marry him
- when I nursed my first child
- when I was published in *Modern Reformation*
- when I signed the contract for my first book

Some of these are more self-explanatory than others. When I took my NTEs I knew I didn't want to be a teacher, but I wanted to have that to fall back on. After all, I had already invested my first three years of college in the education department. And yet six hours of testing made me feel too dumb to even recall my own name. The scores validated my vocation as a college student more than as a teacher. With *Modern Reformation*, that was the first writing I had ever submitted to anything. I thought I'd just test out my thinking and writing skills to see if they would float. But when they published my essay, it was more than a validation to me as a writer. It was an authentication that this organization stood for what they said. I was just a housewife theologian, but they included me in the conversation. It validated for me that these highly educated professors value a housewife theologian. They really were trying to reach ordinary people rather than just talking amongst their academic selves.

We all want validation. Isn't this part of the appeal of some of the reality talent shows? My kids were watching *The Voice* on TV the other day. There is just something about an amazing, undiscovered talent causing competing professional singers to turn their chair for you. I get that knot in my throat when an ordinary person who never knew whether she was good enough belts out a beautiful song in front of who knows how many people.

And maybe this is why some people find it compelling to announce all their accomplishments on social media. "Just power washed the house." "Made the kids bacon, eggs, and hot apple cider for breakfast this morning." "Off to the grocery store . . ." I think the principle "If a tree falls in the forest and no one sees it, does it still make a noise?" is at work here. We have a longing to know that we are in the right place, doing the right thing, for the right purposes.

Most of the time I need to preach to myself that my sufficiency is in Christ, not in how well I can pull off my housewife and writing gig. We know that we aren't working to earn salvation and that our labors should be in grateful response to all Christ has done. I don't make a loaf of homemade bread in order for a great voice from the sky to announce, "Yes, I see the extra effort you put into your calling as a mother and a wife. You may have let them eat Cinnamon Toast Crunch this morning, but they aren't going to have processed bread in their lunchbox today! Way to go!"

Yet in thinking about the emotion that validation brings, I remember that there is a reason for this longing—we *will* be validated in Christ. One day, all those covered in his righteousness will hear, "Well done, good and faithful servant." We crave validation because we should. We hear that blessing every week in the covenant renewal ceremony of Sunday worship. But on that great day, we will hear God himself say that he is pleased with us. And he will be our great reward.

Because of this, I can rest even now in Christ. The preacher to the Hebrews warns them not to be like their ancestors, who rebelled in unbelief even after all God had provided for them in their deliverance. Because of their falling away, God swore they would not enter his rest (3:19). And then he encourages them, "For we who have believed enter that rest" (4:3). In belief we proclaim, "I give up. I give up trying to strive in my own works. It is only in Christ that I am righteous. I trust in Jesus Christ for my salvation. I am validated in him alone. He is good, and he is worthy of my worship. Therefore I can now set out to obey him in my daily life with trust that he is blessing my efforts." We rest in Christ's work. He is the Lord of rest, and I am his.

## REST TO COME

And yet we still struggle in this life. That is the whole reason we need encouragement to persevere. We keep looking to ourselves and need to be reminded of the gospel message. While we know that we can rest in Christ, that our satisfaction is in him, and that God's pleasure for us is because of him, we are still striving in faith to make it to that great day of consummation.

What is this eternal rest that we anticipate? Is it merely inactivity? As we learn about the Sabbath, we see that Christ *is* our rest. In one sense, rest is a place. Verses like Hebrews 4:1, 3–5, 8, and 10 use Greek words that can be translated "abode" or "to colonize."[5] The context here reminds us of the land of Canaan that was to be the Israelite's rest, as well as the rest of God after creation. On Sunday, Christ's covenant community assembles together in a local place for worship. Here we are given Christ and all his benefits.

In another sense, rest is a sort of status. Revelation 14:13 speaks of our future, eternal rest, in contrast to 14:11—the condemned's endless, restless state. The condemned will forever be tormented by their sin. The redeemed will be delivered from suffering. My concordance translates the Greek *rest* from this passage "to repose [be exempt], remain, to refresh, take ease."[6]

Why is this so? Because, unlike Adam, Jesus Christ won for us the new creation and all of its blessings—by his efforts—apart from our efforts. We will be freely active to worship the Lord and serve him, safe in his truth and goodness.

So even in the rest we have now, we are striving for the rest that is to come. It is an active resting in Christ that is equipped with a fighting faith. We long for the rest at the end of the race. And we are given this promise:

> So then, there remains a Sabbath rest for the people of God, for whoever has entered God's rest has also rested from his works as God did from his. (Heb. 4:9–10)

The Greek word used for "Sabbath rest" in this passage, *sabbatismŏs*, is defined as "the repose of Christianity (as a type of heaven):—rest."[7] But the preacher to the Hebrews doesn't want all this talk about resting from our works and looking forward to an eternal rest to lead us to think we should just sit back and take it easy while we wait for the Lord's return. No, he immedi-

5. See James Strong, *The New Strong's Exhaustive Concordance of the Bible* (Nashville: Thomas Nelson Publishers, 1990), Strong's numbers 2663 and 2664.
6. Ibid., Strong's number 373.
7. Ibid., Strong's number 4520.

ately follows, "Let us therefore *strive* to enter that rest, so that no one may fall by the same sort of disobedience" (v. 11). The horror of the Israelites not entering their rest is a warning for all those who profess Christ. His people will be given a fighting faith to finish the race.

Until then, we are called to suffer in this world. We live between the "already" of Christ's victory and the "not yet" of its full consummation. In this tension, believers go through intense training bouts as they take up their cross and follow Christ. We may have already been qualified by the work of Christ, but we are being conditioned for holiness (i.e., sanctified). All the while, we look forward to that day of final jubilee. We will be given our new land where we rest in the efforts of the One who has prepared it for us. Our service to God will continue in our new home—I'm not going to be hanging out on a cloud all day with my formerly deceased pets. But finally I will be able to serve God free from all the constraints caused by the curse. Active rest is freedom in our full recovery to holiness, freedom to fulfill our purpose to glorify God and enjoy him forever.

## SABBATH CONSUMMATION

Occasionally I've heard a well-intentioned Christian trying to counsel a fellow believer who is restless and ready to give up with this popular adage: "You just need to put Jesus in the center of your life!" Let me tell you why that bugs me.

First of all, the picture it creates in my head is picking up one of my son's little action figure guys and placing him in the middle of a circle. That makes me the Unmoved Mover, the controller of who or what gets to be my center. As if Jesus is just anxiously waiting to be promoted from his wingman position (which is reminding me of another bad piece of advice about making him your copilot).

The thing is, Jesus is already the center of everyone's life. For some of us it is a blessed center, and for some it is their greatest destruction. He is our Creator and our Redeemer, "heir of all things" (Heb. 1:2). There's no getting around that, no putting him outside our so-called circle. This is why, if we look to anything else, our life falls apart. There is nothing else worthy of our worship. Think of an axle to a wheel. The wheel cannot properly function as it was invented without a proper axle.

We don't make Jesus the creator of the world, we don't make him heir of all things, and we don't make him our personal Lord and Savior. He is who he is.

The great blessing for us is to have eyes to see and faith to respond, "Here I am."

> Thus, the covenantal self is, to borrow Ricoeur's phrase, "the summoned subject in the school of the narratives of the prophetic vocation." To be human is to be called by God to direct the whole creation to its appointed goal, which is nothing less than sharing in God's Sabbath consummation.[8]

Michael Horton explains that while there is certainly the more narrow vocation of a prophet that we see in Scripture, in a more general sense this is the vocation of every person. All have been given revelation of a Creator God, and we are witnesses as created beings. Even more so, the redeemed are to be witness to God's amazing grace in Jesus Christ. This quote from Horton's *The Christian Faith* is well worth its length.

> To conclude, we come to know ourselves as human beings—that is, as God's image-bearers—not only by looking within but chiefly by looking outside of ourselves to the divine Other who addresses us. It is only as we take our place in this theater of creation—the liturgy of God's speaking and creaturely response—that we discover a selfhood and personhood that is neither autonomous nor illusory but doxological and real. Who am

8. Michael Horton, *The Christian Faith: A Systematic Theology for Pilgrims on the Way* (Grand Rapids: Zondervan, 2011), 405.

I? I am one who exists as a result of being spoken by God. Furthermore, I am one of God's covenant children whom he delivered out of Egypt, sin, and death. I am one who has heard his command but not fulfilled it, one in whom faith has been born by the Spirit through the proclamation of the gospel. Because human beings are by nature created in covenant with God, self-identity itself depends on one's relation to God. It is not because I think, feel, experience, express, observe, or will, but because in the totality of my existence I hear God's command and promise that I recognize that I am, with my fellow image-bearers, a real self who stands in relation to God and the rest of creation.

No one can escape the reality of God in his or her experience, because there is no human existence that is possible or actual apart from the ineradicable covenant identity that belongs to us all, whether we flee the summons, or whether we reply, "Here I am."[9]

God is the one casting us in his great drama. We find our identity and greatest satisfaction in the knowledge and love of our Creator and Redeemer. Our great King has summoned us to appear before him. Jesus has answered the summons, "Here am I, and the children God has given me" (Heb. 2:13 NIV). Therefore, "Let us hold fast the confession of our hope without wavering, for he who promised is faithful" (Heb. 10:23).

For now and for eternity, we can rest on Christ's Word to us. We can rest in his promises, his work, and his covenantal love for his people. As we race together to the finish line, let us also remember that it will be the beginning of a Sabbath consummation. This is the magnificent picture of active rest: living, worshiping, serving, and loving our great God without toil, without sin, in unity together, bearing his image perfectly.

Mahalia Jackson pleaded a songful prayer to the Duke Ellington tune, "Come Sunday." After calling upon our loving,

9. Ibid., 405–6.

almighty Lord above, she asks him to look down on his people and see them through. Her last request and longing is a perfect ending for us all to join in:

> Come Sunday, Oh come Sunday,
> That's the day.[10]

## GOING THE EXTRA MILE

1. Has this chapter changed your thinking about proper rest? For instance, when we consider how the Lord rested after creation, how does that affect your understanding of rest?

2. What is the relationship between rest and fitness, both physically and spiritually? In other words, how does something that seems so counter-productive factor in to our conditioning and stamina?

3. What is your relationship to work? How does the change of the Sabbath from Saturday to Sunday under the new covenant represent the way we should think about work?

4. When you consider the rest that we have now and the eternal rest that is to come, does that make any difference to the way that you view your typical Sunday? What are your thoughts about how we should observe the Sabbath?

5. Do you ever find yourself striving for validation from sources that could never satisfy?

6. How do we *strive* for rest?

7. How is being a "summoned being" related to being in a covenantal relationship with God? What, then, is the significance of theological fitness in this liturgy?

10. Mahalia Jackson, vocal performance of "Come Sunday," by Duke Ellington, recorded 1943, with Duke Ellington, on *Black, Brown, and Beige: Duke Ellington and His Orchestra, Featuring Mahalia Jackson*, Columbia/Legacy /Sony Music Entertainment, 1999, compact disc.

# MORE FROM AIMEE BYRD

Aimee Byrd is determined to reclaim terms like *housewife*, which have divided many women, to unite them instead in their common calling.

What is this calling, and how can women rise above the labels that trap and define them? By taking back another term—*theologian*—and knowing God intimately. Aimee will help you evaluate your Christian life and see your world from a different perspective.

"Aimee Byrd has created a resource that will benefit women tremendously . . . [and] will certainly facilitate some fantastic discussions in your small groups."
  —**Gloria Furman**, Author, *Glimpses of Grace*

"With wisdom, warmth, and wit, Aimee challenges women to think biblically about all of life."
  —**Susan Hunt**, Author, *The True Woman*

"This is a fine book, written with gusto and infectious enthusiasm."
  —**Carl R. Trueman**, Westminster Theological Seminary

# MORE ON CHRISTIAN FITNESS

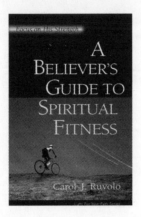

Do you wish you were better fit to handle the challenges of life? This practical guide draws a vivid analogy between physical and spiritual fitness in order to show how God turns our weakness into strength for life and service.

"The principles Carol espouses in these chapters are solidly biblical and eminently practical. Every believer needs a clear understanding of these truths and periodic check-ups regarding their application in daily living."
  **—Georgia Settle**

"How wonderful to find a book that leads us to an understanding of God Himself as the source of spiritual strength. This book is a very helpful guide and companion to all who seek strength to honor God . . . helpful because it is so thoroughly biblical, and a companion because of Carol Ruvolo's tender heart and wise council."
  **—Richard D. Phillips**